Comprehending Test Manuals

A Guide and Workbook

Ann Corwin Silverlake

Pyrczak Publishing
P.O. Box 39731 • Los Angeles, CA 90039

Cover design by Michael Henderson.

Editorial assistance provided by Elaine Fuess, Sharon Young, Brenda Koplin, and Randall R. Bruce.

Printed in the United States of America.
10 9 8 7 6 5 4 3 2   DOC   04 03 02 01 00

ISBN 1-884585-12-4

Table of Contents

Continued→

Introduction

There are many sources of information about tests, but for any given test, the most authoritative is usually its test manual. A manual is the *primary source* of information on the purposes of a test, how it was developed, and how it should be used.

If you will be using tests and measures in your professional work, it is your obligation to thoroughly understand their strengths and limitations. This is especially crucial when you use tests to make important decisions about clients and students. All tests have limitations and shortcomings, and you can learn about many of these by carefully studying their manuals.

Many novices shy away from test manuals because they contain technical information and statistics. Yet, without understanding these parts of the manuals, you are likely to be a poor user of the information obtained with tests. Poor decisions may harm examinees. This book is designed to help you acquire the skills that will make you a professional and competent test user.

The Organization of This Book

Each of the 39 exercises begins with a *Guideline* that briefly reminds you of the important measurement concepts you will need to apply while completing the exercise. The guidelines are only brief reminders since it is assumed that you are using this workbook in conjunction with a comprehensive textbook on tests and measurements. Each guideline also names the statistics, if any, that you will find in the exercise. Review the meanings of these statistics either in your textbook or in Appendix A in this book, which provides a very brief synopsis of each statistic you will need to know.

After each guideline, you will find *Background Notes*. These give you some general information on the test you will be reading about in the excerpt.

The *Excerpt* in each exercise is a direct quotation from a test manual. Each excerpt deals with only a single topic or a group of loosely related topics. This allows easy coordination with your textbook. For example, after you have read about test reliability, your instructor may assign one or more of the exercises on reliability.

Using the Exercises

The exercises may be used as the focus for small-group, in-class activities as well as for homework assignments that are subsequently discussed in class.

Note that some of the exercise questions ask for your opinions. Forming opinions is an essential part of evaluating and selecting tests. Keep in mind, however, that even experts sometimes differ in their opinions on various tests and testing issues. Thus, there may be more than one good answer to some of these questions.

The Tests Represented in This Book

Most of the excerpts were drawn from the manuals for well-known, established tests as well as some lesser-known, new tests. The purpose of this book, however, is *not* to teach you about or endorse any particular tests. Rather, it is to give you systematic practice in reading and interpreting materials in test manuals written by a variety of authors. The skills you learn here can be applied when reading the manuals for any test.

Acknowledgments

I am grateful to the many test publishers who generously granted me permission to reprint portions of their test manuals. Without their cooperation, this book would not have been possible.

Dr. James W. Lichtenberg of the University of Kansas and Dr. Richard Rasor of American River College provided many helpful suggestions on the first draft of this book. Errors and omissions, of course, remain the responsibility of the author.

Ann Corwin Silverlake

Test-Retest Reliability
Behavior Rating Profile[1]

Guideline

Test-retest reliability measures the stability of test scores over time. To estimate this type of reliability, a test is administered twice to a group of examinees—generally with a week or two between the two administrations. The degree of reliability is usually expressed with a correlation coefficient. Note that when a correlation coefficient is used to describe reliability, it is called a "reliability coefficient," or, in this case, a "test-retest reliability coefficient." See Appendix A to review the *correlation coefficient* before attempting this exercise.

Background Notes

The *Behavior Rating Profile*, 2nd edition (BRP-2) is designed for rating students who display disturbed behavior. On one scale, parents rate their children on items such as "Is verbally aggressive to parents" and "Is shy; clings to parents." On another scale, teachers rate the children on items such as "Is an academic underachiever" and "Doesn't follow class rules." On three other scales, children rate themselves in relation to their home lives (e.g., "I often break rules set by my parents"), school lives (e.g., "My teachers give me work that I cannot do"), and peers (e.g., "Other kids don't seem to like me very much.").

Excerpt from the Manual

In the test-retest method, a test is administered to the same group of students on two occasions. A specified period of time is permitted to elapse between administrations, and the results are analyzed to test for mean differences or to determine the correlation of the two sets of data. Kaufman (1980) used this procedure to investigate the stability reliability [i.e., test-retest reliability] of the BRP-2 scales with 36 Indiana high school students, 27 of their parents, and 36 of their teachers, permitting two weeks to intervene between administrations… The resulting coefficients, reported in Table 4.3, range from .78 to .91 with only one coefficient falling below the .80 demarcation. These data provide evidence of the stability of the BRP-2 scales when they are used with adolescents. [See Table 4.3 on the next page.]

---

[1]Brown, L., & Hammill, D. D. (1990). *Examiner's Manual: Behavior Rating Profile* (Second Edition). Austin, TX: Pro-Ed. Excerpt reprinted with permission. Copyright © 1990 by Pro-Ed.

Table 4.3 *Delayed Test-Retest Reliability of
the BRP-2 Scales with Adolescents
(decimals omitted)*

BRP-2 Scale	r
Parent Rating Scale	84
Teacher Rating Scale	91
Student Rating Scales: Home	78
Student Rating Scales: School	83
Student Rating Scales: Peer	86

Questions:

1. Which one of the scales is the most reliable? Explain.

2. Which one of the scales is the least reliable? Explain.

3. In your opinion, are all the scales adequately reliable? Explain.

4. The excerpt presents the results of only one of a number of reliability studies described in the manual for the BRP-2. In your opinion, is this one study sufficient or are others needed? Explain.

5. In Table 4.3, decimals have been omitted. If they were *not* omitted, what would the reliability coefficient be for the Parent Rating Scale?

6. The test-retest reliability coefficients are based on a two-week interval. Do you think the coefficients would be higher *or* lower if a two-month interval had been used? Explain.

7. Speculate on why test makers usually allow an interval of a week or two between the two administrations of the test instead of giving the same test twice in a row at one sitting.

8. If you were considering using this instrument, what other types of reliability coefficients, if any, would you like to see in the manual? Explain.

9. In general, how important is test-retest reliability information for selecting a scale or test? Would you consider it a serious flaw if a manual did not contain information on this topic? Explain.

10. If you have a measurement textbook, do the authors suggest a minimum acceptable value for a test-retest reliability coefficient? If yes, what is it? If yes, do all of the coefficients in the excerpt exceed the minimum value?

Interscorer Reliability

Wechsler Preschool and Primary Scale of Intelligence[1]

Guideline

Scoring some tests involves making subjective judgments. For example, some subjectivity often enters into scoring essays, and, as a result, one English teacher might give an essay a grade of A while another might give it a grade of B. Such a lack of agreement indicates a weakness in interscorer reliability (i.e., the consistency of scores from one scorer to another).

Interscorer reliability is usually judged by having a set of examinees' responses to the test scored by two or more scorers and correlating the two sets of scores by computing a correlation coefficient. Note that when a correlation coefficient is used for this purpose, it is called an "interscorer reliability coefficient." See Appendix A to review the *correlation coefficient* before attempting this exercise.

Background Notes

The Wechsler Preschool and Primary Scale of Intelligence–Revised (WPPSI-R) is an individually administered intelligence test for young children. The test administrator observes an individual examinee's responses and scores them.

Excerpt from the Manual

Most WPPSI-R subtests involve straightforward and quite objective scoring; however, some subtests are subjectively scored, and are therefore more vulnerable to scoring error. For these subtests, which include Comprehension, Vocabulary, Similarities, and Mazes, it was necessary to evaluate interscorer reliability. In addition, previous research with the WPPSI indicated a low rate of scoring agreement on the Geometric Design subtest (Sattler, 1976). A more objective set of scoring rules and procedures was created for this subtest, and its effect on scorer agreement also was evaluated.

To assess the interscorer reliability of the Comprehension, Vocabulary, Similarities, and Mazes subtests, a sample of 151 cases (83 males and 68 females) stratified by age was randomly selected from all cases collected for the standardization. For the Geometric Design subtest, a sample of 188 cases (105 males and 83 females) was randomly selected. A group of research scorers was trained and given practice in scoring the subtests. The cases were subdivided by age to control for age effects, and two scorers were selected at random to score all the cases in each age group.

To ensure that scorings were independent, any previous scoring notations on standardization Record Forms were masked, leaving only the verbatim responses on the Verbal subtests, the performance times and tracing on Mazes, and the actual drawings on

---

Geometric Design. Scorers in the study recorded their scores on separate forms so that they never saw each other's scores. . . .

Interscorer reliability coefficients were as follows: .96 on Comprehension, .94 on Vocabulary, .96 on Similarities, .94 on Mazes, and .88 on Geometric Design. These results indicate that the scoring rules for these subtests are objective enough for different scorers to produce similar results.

Questions:

1. Why was scorer agreement examined for only some of the WPPSI-R subtests?

2. Cases were selected at random. What is random selection?

3. Cases were selected from all cases collected for the standardization. What do you think the "standardization" is?

4. Is it important to know that the research scorers were trained and given practice in scoring the subtests? Explain.

5. How many scorers scored the cases in each age group? In your opinion, is this an adequate number?

6. The responses had been previously scored. Is it important to know that the research scorers were not allowed to see the previous scoring notations? Why? Why not?

7. Is it important to know that the research scorers did not see each other's scores? Why? Why not?

8. On which subtest was the interscorer reliability the lowest? Explain.

9. Overall, do you think that the interscorer reliability is adequate? Explain.

EXERCISE 3

Internal Consistency and Test-Retest Reliability

Occupational Aptitude Survey and Interest Schedule[1]

Guideline

Coefficient alpha (expressed from 0.00 to 1.00) indicates the extent to which, on the average, all the items in a test are correlated with each other. A high value (near 1.00) indicates a high degree of consistency from item to item in what the test is measuring. Some test makers regard it as a measure of reliability since it indicates the extent to which different sets of items within the same test would yield the same results. Others regard it as a "measure of internal consistency." The coefficient is often called "Cronbach's alpha" in recognition of Lee Cronbach, who proposed it.

See Exercise 1 for a description of test-retest reliability. See Appendix A to review the *median* and *correlation coefficient* before attempting this exercise.

Background Notes

The *Interest Schedule* (IS) is part of the *Occupational Aptitude Survey and Interest Schedule* (OASIS-2). It measures occupational interest in areas such as Artistic, Scientific, and Mechanical. It was developed as a career guidance tool for use in occupational counseling.

Excerpt from the Manual

Alpha reliability provides an index of inter-item consistency, that is, item homogeneity or unidimensionality. A test composed of items that measure the same unitary construct would be expected to have a high degree of alpha reliability. . . . Alpha reliability is based on one administration of a test (Anastasi, 1988).

. . . test-retest reliability requires two administrations of a test. This form of reliability is obtained by administering the same test at two different times, usually separated by 1 or 2 weeks, and correlating the resulting scores. Test-retest reliability measures stability of the test scores over time (Anastasi, 1988).

Tables 5 and 6 present alpha reliabilities for 260 students in Grade 8, 10, and 12, and for 177 males and females, respectively.

Table 5 reveals alpha coefficients ranging from .78 to .94. The median coefficients for the 12 scales range from .86 to .94. Table 6 contains alpha coefficients ranging from .85 to .95. The coefficients in Tables 5 and 6 indicate that the IS has sufficient reliability...

The test-retest reliability with a 2-week interval computed on data from 54 junior high and high school students for the 12 OASIS-2 IS subscales in the order in which the scales are scored [listed in Tables 5 and 6] was .91, .77, .75, .81, .72, .75, .88, .66, .89, .82, .86, and .90, respectively. These figures suggest that the IS scales are relatively stable over time.

---

[1]Parker, R. M. (1991). *Examiner's Manual: Occupational Aptitude Survey and Interest Schedule.* Austin, TX: Pro-Ed. Copyright © 1991 by Pro-Ed. Reprinted with permission.

Table 5 *Alpha Reliability Coefficients for the 12 OASIS-2 IS Scales for 260 Students in Grades 8, 10, and 12*

IS Scale	Total	Grade			Median
		8	10	12	
1. Artistic	89	90	88	87	88
2. Scientific	90	92	88	89	89
3. Nature	94	92	94	94	94
4. Protective	91	91	91	91	91
5. Mechanical	92	93	90	92	92
6. Industrial	90	90	89	87	89
7. Business Detail	91	90	92	92	92
8. Selling	89	89	89	87	89
9. Accommodating	85	86	86	78	86
10. Humanitarian	89	88	91	87	88
11. Leading-Influencing	88	88	87	87	87
12. Physical Performing	90	89	90	89	89
Number of students	260	86	112	62	

Editor's Note: Only the relevant portions of the table are shown here.

Table 6 *Alpha Reliability Coefficients on the OASIS-2 IS for 177 Students in Grades 8-12 Grouped by Sex*

IS Scale	Sex	
	Female	Male
1. Artistic	89	88
2. Scientific	88	93
3. Nature	91	95
4. Protective	92	91
5. Mechanical	89	89
6. Industrial	90	89
7. Business Detail	89	88
8. Selling	89	91
9. Accommodating	85	87
10. Humanitarian	88	89
11. Leading-Influencing	87	88
12. Physical Performing	89	89
N	84	93

Note: All decimals have been deleted.

Questions:

1. According to the excerpt, which type of reliability requires only one administration of a test?

2. The excerpt states that a test measuring a "unitary construct" would be expected to have a high degree of alpha reliability. Would a scale that measures both artistic interests and mechanical interests and yields a single score for the combined interests be an example of a "unitary construct"? Explain.

3. According to Table 5, which IS scale has the highest alpha at grade 12?

4. According to Table 5, *on the average* across grade levels, which IS scale has the highest alpha?

5. In your opinion, are the values of alpha in Table 6 similar for females and males? Explain.

6. According to the excerpt, how many weeks usually separate the two administrations of a test in order to estimate test-retest reliability? If you have a tests and measurements textbook, check to see if this interval is appropriate according to your textbook authors and write your finding here.

7. The test-retest reliability is lowest for which IS scale?

8. The test-retest reliability is highest for which IS scale?

9. On the whole, are the alpha reliabilities or the test-retest reliabilities higher?

10. Since the test-retest reliabilities and the alphas are based on different samples, are they strictly comparable? Explain.

11. If you wanted to know whether the IS scores would be similar if the test was administered to examinees at different times, which type of reliability would give you better information?

12. Are there any other types of reliability estimates you would like to see for the IS? Explain.

EXERCISE 4

Internal Consistency Reliability (Cronbach's Alpha)

The Sixteen Personality Factor Questionnaire[1]

Guideline

See the Guideline for Exercise 3 to review Cronbach's alpha reliability. *Split-half* reliability, which is also mentioned in this exercise, is determined by correlating two halves of the test with each other. For example, we can get a score for each examinee by scoring only the odd-numbered items. Then we can get another score for each examinee by scoring only the even-numbered items. By correlating the two sets of scores, we can determine the extent to which the halves of the test yield consistent results.

See Appendix A to review the *mean* and the *correlation coefficient* before attempting this exercise.

Background Notes

The Sixteen Factor Personality Questionnaire (16PF) measures 16 primary components of personality: Warmth, Reasoning, Emotional Stability, Dominance, Liveliness, Rule-Consciousness, Social Boldness, Sensitivity, Vigilance, Abstractedness, Privateness, Apprehension, Openness to Change, Self-Reliance, Perfectionism, and Tension. Combinations of the 16 scales can be used to get scores on Extroversion, Anxiety, Tough-Mindedness, Independence, and Self-Control.

Excerpt from the Manual

Internal Consistency

In contrast to test-retest information, internal consistency can be viewed as reliability estimated from a single test administration.

Measurement of the internal reliability of a test provides a source of evidence that all items in a given scale assess the same construct. As the intercorrelations among items within a scale increase, reliability of the scale itself increases. Internal consistency is lowered to the degree that items on the same scale measure different traits or to the extent that scale items are not intercorrelated.

As a measure of scale internal consistency, Cronbach's coefficient alpha essentially calculates the average value of all possible split-half reliabilities (Cronbach, 1951). Cronbach alpha coefficients for the 16PF Fifth Edition were calculated on the general population norm sample of 2,500 adults. Values ranged from .64 (Openness to Change, Factor Q1) to .85 (Social Boldness, Factor H), with an average of .74 (see Table 10).

---

[1]Russell, M. & Karol, D. (1994). *Administrator's Manual* for the *16PF–Fifth Edition*. Copyright © 1994 by the Institute for Personality and Ability Testing, Inc. Reproduced with permission. "16PF" is a registered trademark belonging to the Institute for Personality and Ability Testing.

Table 10 *Internal Reliability Data (Cronbach Coefficient Alpha) (Based on Norm Sample, N = 2,500)*

Factor		Alpha
A	Warmth	.69
B	Reasoning	.77
C	Emotional Stability	.78
E	Dominance	.66
F	Liveliness	.72
G	Rule-Consciousness	.75
H	Social Boldness	.85
I	Sensitivity	.77
L	Vigilance	.74
M	Abstractedness	.74
N	Privateness	.75
O	Apprehension	.78
Q1	Openness to Change	.64
Q2	Self-Reliance	.78
Q3	Perfectionism	.71
Q4	Tension	.76
	Mean	.74

Note: From "Reliability and Equivalency: Comparison of the 16PF Fifth Edition and Fourth Edition (Form A)" by S. R. Conn, 1994. In S. R. Conn & M L. Rieke (Eds.) *The 16PF Fifth Edition Technical Manual*. Champaign, IL: Institute for Personality and Ability Testing, Inc.

Questions:

1. What is the value of alpha for Abstractedness?

2. Which factor has the highest alpha?

3. Which factor has the lowest internal consistency?

4. What is the average value of alpha for all the factors?

5. If you have a tests and measurements book, examine it to see if the authors give recommended minimum values for alpha. If so, do all of the factors in the 16PF meet the minimum standards?

6. If you want to know how stable the scores are over time, does alpha provide the information you need? Explain.

7. If you have a tests and measurements textbook, examine the material on the split-half method and Cronbach's alpha. Do the authors prefer one over the other? Explain.

8. In your opinion, how important is it for a test manual to include values of Cronbach alpha? (You may wish to examine your textbook before answering this question.)

9. Suppose you examined the manual for a different set of scales and found that the values of Cronbach's alpha were consistently low (such as all below .30). What would this tell you about the scales?

10. If a test manual only provided values of Cronbach and did not provide other reliability information, would this be sufficient? (You may wish to examine your textbook before answering this question.)

EXERCISE 5

Concurrent Validity and Test-Retest Reliability

Reading and Arithmetic Indexes (12)[1]

Guideline

To determine the *criterion-related validity* of a test, we correlate examinees' scores on the test with their scores on a "criterion measure." For example, to validate a new reading test, we might correlate scores students earn on this test with their teachers' ratings of their reading ability, with the teachers' ratings being the criterion (or standard) by which we will judge the validity of the test. The resulting correlation coefficient is called a *validity coefficient*.

There are two types of criterion-related validity: *concurrent* and *predictive*. In this exercise and Exercise 6, you will be reading about concurrent validity. In this type, the test scores and the criterion measurements are collected at about the same time; hence, we use the word *concurrent*, which means "at the same time." Predictive validity will be covered in Exercise 7.

A test-retest reliability coefficient indicates the extent to which the scores of individuals remain in the same order when they take a test twice. See the Guideline for Exercise 1 for more information on this type of reliability.

See Appendix A to review the *correlation coefficient* before attempting this exercise.

Background Notes

The Reading and Arithmetic Indexes (12) (RAI-12) are multiple-choice tests designed for use with applicants for entry-level jobs and special training programs.[2] The tests are at a more basic level than most other selection tests, which often are designed for applicants for higher-level jobs. The Reading Index has six parts, ranging from "picture-word association" to "comprehension of paragraphs." The Arithmetic Index has six parts, ranging from "addition and subtraction of whole numbers" to "basic operations involving geometry and word problems."

Excerpt from the Manual

Validity and Reliability

As indicated in Table 1, the initial validity and reliability of the RAI (12) was established in several settings... The RAI (12) was administered to three groups, office clerical employees of a national insurance company, manufacturing employees of a national food products organization, and vocational students from several schools across the United States. As shown in Table 1, the reliabilities for the RAI (12) were high. The RAI (12) was very predictive of [on-the-job] performance for each of the concurrent

---

[1]SRA (1995). *Examiner's Manual: Reading and Arithmetic Indexes (12)*. Copyright © 1995 by McGraw-Hill/London House. Reprinted with permission.

[2]The *12* in the title of the test indicates that this edition of the test is suitable for skill levels through grade 12.

validity studies shown. Overall, RAI (12) is both a reliable and valid predictor of performance for education and job-oriented behavior.

Table 1   *Validity/Reliability of RAI (12)*

Test	Group	N	Reliability (test-retest)	Validity	Criterion
Arithmetic	Office/Clerical	103	.89	.41	Performance
	Vocational Students	141	.93	.33	Grade-Point Average
	Manufacturing Employees	72	.84	.39	Performance
Reading	Office/Clerical	98	.88	.38	Performance
	Vocational Students	136	.91	.34	Grade-Point Average
	Manufacturing Employees	74	.86	.40	Performance

*All p values < .01

Questions:

1. How many examinees were in the office/clerical sample for the Reading Test?

2. In your opinion, are the sample sizes adequate? Explain.

3. Which Test/Group combination had the highest reliability coefficient?

4. Which Test/Group combination had the lowest reliability coefficient?

5. In your opinion, do the results in the table support the claim that the RAI (12) has adequate reliability?

6. Which Test/Group combination had the highest validity coefficient?

7. Which Test/Group combination had the lowest validity coefficient?

8. In your opinion, do the results in the table support the claim that the RAI (12) has adequate validity?

9. Suppose an admissions officer at a vocational school planned to use the RAI (12) as the sole basis for making decisions on which students were to be admitted. On the basis of the statistics in the table, should the officer expect that this test would let in some students who will not do well in the school? Should the officer expect that this test would keep out some students who would have done well if admitted? Do you think that the officer should supplement the RAI (12) with other types of information? Explain.

10. Overall, the reliability coefficients for the RAI (12) are higher than the validity coefficients. If you have a tests and measurements textbook, examine it to see if the author(s) suggest whether this is typical for most tests. Write your findings here.

11. The excerpt shows the entire section in the manual on reliability and validity. Note, however, that the authors invite users of the test to conduct additional studies, which the publisher will share with all users. Do you think additional studies are needed? Explain.

EXERCISE 6

Concurrent Validity

Thurstone Test of Mental Alertness[1]

Guideline

See Exercise 5 to review concurrent validity.

See Appendix A to review the *mean, standard deviation, correlation coefficient,* and *statistical significance* before attempting this exercise.

Background Notes

The Thurstone Test of Mental Alertness (TMA) is designed to measure general mental ability. It consists of four types of multiple-choice items: (1) arithmetic reasoning (solving arithmetic word problems), (2) number series (determining which number comes next in a series such as 5, 10, 15, __?__), (3) same-opposite meaning (vocabulary items in which examinees identify a choice that has either the same or opposite meaning as a word), and (4) definitions (reading a definition and identifying the word being defined).

The author recommends the test for use in educational or industrial settings to answer questions such as "Will the student be able to understand complex material?" and "Does the applicant have the capacity to learn the job requirements?"

Excerpt from the Manual

High correlations between the TMA [and] school grades…were found. This indicates the TMA can identify students of different ability and performance levels and is also a good predictor of academic success.

Correlations with Student Grades

Two studies compared the TMA scores and student grade point averages. In the first study, the TMA was administered to ninth-grade students in three different areas of the United States. School A was located in an industrial town in Alabama, School B in a fruit-growing region of California, and School C in a mining area of the Southwest. High correlations between the TMA and grade point were found. The results are shown in Table 7.

The second study involved twelfth-grade students in Schools A, B, and C above and a fourth School D in Pennsylvania. The correlations, means and standard deviations are given in Table 8.

The school grades were obtained during the same school semester that the tests were given in the above studies. The median validity in these studies is .64.

---

[1]Thurstone, L. L. & Thurstone, T. G. (1996). *Examiner's Manual: Thurstone Test of Mental Alertness.* Copyright © 1996 by McGraw-Hill/London House. Reprinted with permission.

Table 7 Correlations of TMA Total Score and Grade Point Average for
Ninth-Grade Students

			TMA Total Score		Grade Point Average	
Group	N	Correlation	Mean	Standard Deviation	Mean	Standard Deviation
School A	151	.70**	39.90	15.41	1.71	1.20
School B	383	.57**	36.66	18.99	2.29	0.20
School C	225	.66**	41.87	15.23	1.89	0.79

Note: In this and the following table: **$p < .01$

Table 8 Correlations of TMA Total Score and Grade Point Average for
Twelfth-Grade Students

			TMA Total Score		Grade Point Average	
Group	N	Correlation	Mean	Standard Deviation	Mean	Standard Deviation
School A	93	.61**	55.12	15.02	2.58	0.93
School B	214	.77**	51.60	19.82	2.51	0.80
School C	106	.40**	50.92	13.44	2.18	0.47
School D	132	.64**	50.64	16.07		

Editor's Note: The means and standard deviations of the grade point averages for School D
in Table 8 are not given in the test manual.

Questions:

1. How many twelfth-grade students in School C were tested?

2. For the twelfth-grade students, which school had the highest average TMA score?

3. For the ninth-grade students, which school had the most variation in their TMA scores?

4. For the ninth-grade students, which school had the least variation in their grade point averages?

5. The concurrent validity was highest for ninth-grade students in which school?

6. The concurrent validity was highest for twelfth-grade students in which school?

7. The concurrent validity was lowest for twelfth-grade students in which school?

8. If you square a correlation coefficient, multiply by 100, and add a % sign, you get the percentage of "variance accounted for." (See Appendix A for more information on

this topic.) This indicates, in terms of a percentage, the extent to which the differences in grade-point averages are accounted for by the TMA scores. What is the percentage of variance in grade-point averages accounted for by the correlation for School B for twelfth-grade students?

9. What is the percentage of variance in grade point averages accounted for by the TMA scores for twelfth-grade students in School C?

10. The footnote to Table 7 says that "**$p < .01$." Explain in your own words what this means.

11. Overall, what is your impression of the validity of the TMA based on the information in the tables?

12. In the manual, there are additional validity studies in which TMA scores are correlated with other test scores and measures of performance in industrial settings. However, the only studies correlating TMA scores with grades are included in the excerpt. Do you think that it would be a good idea for the test maker to conduct additional studies in which TMA scores are correlated with grade point averages? Why? Why not?

13. A principle in measurement is that a given test can be more valid for some types of students than for others. Does the excerpt illustrate this principle? Explain.

Predictive Validity

Wechsler Intelligence Scale for Children[1]

Guideline

Because the major purpose of intelligence tests is to predict achievement, the correlation between intelligence test scores (IQs) and achievement is frequently examined to estimate predictive validity. In such studies, the achievement measure is called the "criterion."[2] (The word *criterion* means *standard*; thus, we are using the prediction of achievement as the standard for judging the validity of an IQ test.) Correlation coefficients in predictive validity studies are usually positive in value, ranging from 0.00 (no validity) to 1.00 (perfect validity).[3] See Appendix A to review the *median, correlation coefficient* and *percentage of variance accounted for* before attempting this exercise.

Background Notes

The Wechsler Intelligence Scale for Children–Third Edition (WISC-R) is a popular individual intelligence test. It yields a Verbal IQ (VIQ) based on subscales such as information, arithmetic, and comprehension; a Performance IQ (PIQ) based on subscales such as picture completion, object assembly; and block design, as well as a Full Scale IQ, (FSIQ) which is based on a combination of the Verbal and Performance scales.

Excerpt from the Manual

Prediction of Academic Achievement

Numerous studies have been conducted to investigate the relationship between the WISC-R and a variety of achievement tests. Representative results are highlighted here, and Sattler (1988) provides a useful summary of results for more than 40 studies of WISC-R criterion validity. Median correlations across studies of the WISC-R and the *Wide Range Achievement Test* (WRAT; Jastak & Jastak, 1978) reading scores, for example were .57 for the Verbal scale and .56 for the Full Scale. WRAT Arithmetic scores showed median correlations of .62 with the Verbal scale and .52 with the Full Scale. Both [the reading and arithmetic] WRAT scores had lower correlations with the Performance scale (.34 and .46, respectively). Summarizing other achievement test results, Sattler (1988) reported median correlations of .66, .47, and .65 for the VIQ, PIQ, and FSIQ scores respectively, with reading scores, and median correlations of .56, .48, and .58, respectively

---

[1]*Wechsler Intelligence Scale for Children–Third Edition.* Copyright © 1990 by The Psychological Corporation. Reproduced by permission. All rights reserved. "Wechsler Intelligence Scale for Children" and "WISC-III" are registered trademarks of The Psychological Corporation.

[2]When we determine how well test scores predict some criterion, the study is often called a "predictive validity study." Predictive validity is a type of criterion-related validity. The other type is "concurrent validity," which is discussed in Exercises 5 and 6.

[3]Sometimes they are negative, varying between 0.00 and −1.00. For example, if you correlate scores on an anxiety scale that yields *higher* scores for highly anxious individuals with scores on another anxiety scale that yields *lower* scores for highly anxious individuals, you would expect a negative correlation. When discussing validity, "correlation coefficients" are often called "validity coefficients."

respectively, with reading scores, and median correlations of .56, .48, and .58, respectively for arithmetic scores. A study by Reynolds, Wright, and Dappen (1981), not included in Sattler's summary, showed a higher correlation (.60) between the WRAT Arithmetic and WISC-R Full Scale than for the WRAT Reading and Full Scale (.36).

Questions:

1. Briefly define the term "median correlation."

2. The *median* correlation between WRAT reading scores and WISC-III Verbal IQ is reported in the excerpt as .57. In light of the meaning of the "median," what percentage of the correlation coefficients was lower than .57?

3. What percentage of the variance is accounted for by the correlation in question 2?

4. The sixth sentence in the excerpt, beginning with "Summarizing other . . . ," contains six correlations. Organize them in the following table by writing their values in the appropriate spaces. One of the correlations has been entered for you.

Table for Question 4   *Correlations between WISC-III scores and achievement scores*

	Reading Scores	Arithmetic Scores
VIQ Scores	.66	
PIQ Scores		
FSIQ Scores		

5. According to the values in the table you filled in for question 4, are the Verbal IQ scores a better predictor of reading scores *or* arithmetic scores? Explain.

6. According to the values in the table you filled in for question 4, which type of IQ score (VIQ, PIQ, *or* FSIQ) is the best predictor of arithmetic scores? Explain.

7. Using the information in the table for question 4, calculate the percentage of the variance on arithmetic scores accounted for by the Full Scale IQ.

8. Of all the validity coefficients reported in the excerpt, which one is lowest in value? What percentage of the variance is accounted for by this correlation coefficient?

9. Of all the validity coefficients reported in the excerpt, which one is the highest in value? What percentage of the variance is accounted for by this correlation coefficient?

10. Based on the excerpt, do you think that the WISC-III is reasonably valid? Would it be a good idea to examine the validity data in the manuals for other tests before selecting this test for use with children? Explain.

EXERCISE 8

Content Validity: I

Test of Written Language[1]

Guideline

One way to estimate the validity of a test is to examine its contents. For example, we might judge the content validity of a tenth-grade history test by comparing what is on the test with the tenth-grade history objectives adopted by a school district. To the extent that the test reflects and measures attainment of the objectives, the test has content validity for the tenth-graders in this school. More information on this approach to validity is included in the excerpt.

Background Notes

The Test of Written Language–Third Edition (TOWL-3) is a comprehensive test for evaluating written language. It is designed for use with ages 7 through 17. One of its subtests is described below in the excerpt.

Excerpt from the Manual

Content validity involves the "systematic examination of the test content to determine whether it covers a representative sample of the behavior domain to be measured" (Anastasi, 1988, p. 140). Obviously, this kind of validity has to be built into the test when the subtests are conceptualized and the items are constructed. Test builders usually address content validity by showing . . . that the abilities chosen to be measured are consistent with the current knowledge about a particular area. . . .

Subtest 1: Vocabulary
Description: *The student writes a sentence that incorporates a stimulus word.*

A common way of measuring writing vocabulary is to have students define the meanings of words that they have read. Although this is an important ability, we believe that the actual use of vocabulary in sentence construction is more relevant to everyday reality. We have noted that students frequently use words properly in sentences because they have *some* idea, if not the exact idea, of what the word means. For example, some students who may not know that the word *effete* means "wasted" may use the word correctly in a sentence because they know that it is usually a derogatory term and they wish to express a derogatory thought at the time. Also, there is more to words than their dictionary meanings. Semantically speaking, words belong to classes, and a student who intuitively knows a word's class should be able to generate a meaningful sentence that includes that word, without knowing the precise meaning. To illustrate, the student who says or writes, "The boy is effete," demonstrates a vocabulary knowledge well beyond the one who might say or write, "Effete ran to town" or "The boy has effete." [*Editor's note:*

[1]Hammill, D. D. & Larsen, S. C. (1996). *Examiner's Manual: Test of Written Language–Third Edition.* Austin, TX: Pro-Ed. Copyright © 1996 by Pro-Ed. Reprinted with permission.

In light of this rationale, points are given on the TOWL-3 Vocabulary subtest for using each word in a meaningful sentence.]

Having chosen a testing format, we next selected the words to serve as items. We wanted to select words that were used in school, that included all parts of speech, and that did not represent specific vocabularies such as science and social studies. To accomplish this, three widely used reading word lists were consulted: the *Basic Elementary Reading Vocabularies* (Harris & Jacobson, 1972), the *EDL Core Vocabularies in Reading, Mathematics, Science, and Social Studies* (Taylor, et al., 1979), and *A Teacher's Word Book of 30,000 Words* (Thorndike & Lorge, 1944). Thorndike and Lorge's list is a combination of words that appear in all kinds of written material. The other two lists comprise words that are included in popular basal reading series and/or on word-frequency lists. The use of these lists ensured that the words selected for inclusion on the subtest would have importance in determining instructional levels relative to general school reading material.

Next, we had to choose which particular words on these lists should be selected to serve as items on the subtest. This was accomplished by randomly selecting words that were at the same grade level across all three lists. If a word from a special vocabulary was selected (e.g., *divisor, ozone, latitude*) another word was chosen.

Questions:

1. The item or testing format is part of the contents of a test. What is your opinion on the format used in the TOWL-3 for measuring vocabulary? Do you think it is a more valid way to measure vocabulary than having examinees define words?

2. Is there an advantage to using word lists based on popular basal reading series (i.e., a series of structured reading books used for reading instruction)? Explain.

3. The *Teacher's Word Book of 30,000 Words* is old. Is this a problem? Explain.

4. The test makers selected words at random from the lists (with certain restrictions). In your opinion, is there an advantage to doing this? Would it have been better for them to use their subjective judgment to select words they thought would be most valid for use on the test?

5. If it was at grade level 3 on one list and at grade level 5 on the other lists, was the word eligible for inclusion on the test?

6. The excerpt says if a word was from a "special vocabulary," it was not included in the test. Explain what you think the test makers mean by the term "special vocabulary."

7. Do you think it was a good idea to omit words from a "special vocabulary"?

8. Is there anything you would like to know about the content validity of the Vocabulary Subtest that is not included in the excerpt? Explain.

9. Based on the excerpt, what is your overall opinion on the content validity of the Vocabulary Subtest of the TOWL-3?

10. Suppose you were a middle-school science teacher building a test on the scientific vocabulary covered in your science textbook. Furthermore, suppose there were more than a hundred scientific terms in the textbook, but you wanted to sample only 20 of them for your test. How would you select the 20 terms to include on your test? Would your method ensure that your test has high content validity?

EXERCISE 9

Content Validity: II
Boehm Test of Basic Concepts[1]

Guideline

See Exercise 8 to review the meaning of content validity.

Background Notes

The Boehm Test of Basic Concepts–Revised Edition (Boehm-R) is "designed to assess beginning school children's knowledge of frequently used basic concepts that are sometimes mistakenly assumed to be familiar to children at the time of entry into kindergarten or first grade." A major purpose is to identify children who may be "at risk" for learning because their overall concept level is low. The test covers concepts such as distance, size, numerical order, and names of common objects.

In the excerpt, the First Edition of the test is referred to as the BTBC.

Excerpt from the Manual

Sources of Content Validity

In preparing the content for the Boehm-R, the importance of concepts assessed on the BTBC was reexamined in relation to the frequency of the 50 target terms in (a) printed materials, (b) reading and mathematics curricula, and (c) teachers' verbal instructions (Boehm, Kaplan, & Preddy, 1980).

Print Materials

Of the 50 target terms assessed on the BTBC, 41 appeared among the 1,000 most used words in the Thorndike-Lorge *Teacher's Wordbook of 30,000 Words* (1944) obtained from adult and juvenile printed materials. Of these concepts, 34 were among the 500 most frequently appearing words. The Boehm-R includes 8 new concepts, 5 of which are among the 500 most frequently appearing words.

Although the Thorndike-Lorge list continues to be widely referenced, its datedness might be questioned for present-day reading materials for children. A more recent study of basal reading series was conducted to establish a core vocabulary for the Educational Development Laboratories' (EDL) language arts programs (Taylor, Franckenpohl, & White, 1979). All except four of the BTBC (three of the Boehm-R) terms appeared in the reading materials for kindergarten to Grade 3. (The terms that did not appear are *medium-sized, separated*, and *backward*.)

Based on these two sources, it can be concluded that the terms assessed by the Boehm-R are necessary for early development of reading skills.

---

[1]Boehm, A. E. (1986). Manual from the *Boehm Test of Basic Concepts–Revised*. San Antonio: The Psychological Corporation. Copyright © 1986 by The Psychological Corporation. Reproduced by permission. All rights reserved.

Curriculum Content

In view of the fact that curricular materials change over time, the original survey on which the BTBC was based (Boehm, 1967) was repeated (Boehm et al., 1980). A twenty-page random sample of words to be read by the teacher or child was drawn from the workbooks of five major reading series and five major mathematics series at kindergarten, Grade 1, and Grade 2. All of the original BTBC terms were…[found in the workbooks] as well as synonym, antonym, and comparative forms of these terms…

Teachers' Verbal Instructions

The child's ability to use basic concepts is essential not only to school learning in general, but also to following teachers' verbal directions. The characteristics of oral directions given by classroom teachers, as well as children's ability to follow them, was studied by Kaplan (1979) and Kaplan and White (1980). An analysis of the oral directions given by 18 kindergarten through Grade 5 teachers in the Kaplan study revealed that these teachers presented directions at the rate of 1.4 per minute. The directions presented related to both academic work and classroom management. Directions consisted of behaviors to be followed such as "Sit down," and qualifiers of these behaviors such as "Sit down in the front row." The complexity of the directions used was generally stable across grades. Of the terms defined as qualifiers used by these teachers, 41% were the same as those assessed by the BTBC. According to Kaplan and White (1980), many of the remaining qualifiers clearly resemble Boehm's relational words.

A reanalysis of these transcripts for kindergarten through Grade 2 teachers (Boehm et al.1980) revealed that of the 711 verbal directions presented, BTBC terms were used frequently, at a rate of .56 BTBC terms and .36 synonyms and antonyms of these terms, for a total of .92 concept terms per teacher direction (.65 Boehm-R concepts and .27 synonyms and antonyms were used per teacher direction). In addition to the use of the BTBC concepts reported, teachers in these three grades frequently used easier relational concepts such as *up-down, big-little,* and *tall-short.* It can be concluded, therefore, that the basic concepts assessed by the test are used frequently in teachers' verbal directions.

These sources support the claim that the child's ability to make relational judgments using the BTBC concept terms, plus their synonyms and antonyms, is basic to understanding classroom instruction, whether in the form of following teacher directions, completing curricular tasks, or reading text.

Questions:

1. In your opinion, how serious is the "datedness" of the Thorndike-Lorge list for validating concepts such as "between," "inside," and "equal," which are covered by the Boehm-R? Do you think that they are any more or less important for school children to know today than they were a half century ago?

2. In your opinion, is the fact that all the BTBC terms were included in the sample of workbooks important for establishing the test's validity? Explain.

3. In addition to the workbooks, are there other types of written materials that children are exposed to in school that might be analyzed to identify important concepts to cover in this type of test?

4. The terms *up-down*, *big-little*, and *tall-short* were not included in the BTBC because they were found to be easy—even though teachers frequently use these terms. Is it appropriate to exclude very easy material when building a test? Explain.

5. The contents of verbal instructions given by 18 teachers were used to help estimate the validity of the test. In your opinion, is a sample of 18 sufficient? Would you like to know more about these teachers? Explain.

6. On a scale from 1 (very little) to 5 (very much), how much confidence do you have in the validity of the Boehm-R based on the information in the excerpt about its content validity? Explain.

7. Suppose the test maker had correlated the scores on the Boehm-R given at the beginning of kindergarten with the scores obtained on a reading test given at the end of first grade. Would the information obtained from such a study be an important supplement to the information on content validity given in the excerpt? Explain.

EXERCISE 10

Construct Validity: I

Comprehensive Receptive and Expressive Vocabulary Test[1]

Guideline

A hypothetical construct such as *cheerfulness* stands for a collection of related behaviors such as "smiles frequently," "laughs easily," and so on. We can estimate the construct validity of a cheerfulness scale by administering it to a sample of individuals and then checking to see whether their scores "make sense" in terms of our theoretical and everyday notions of "cheerfulness." For example, did the individuals who have more friends score higher on our cheerfulness scale than those who have fewer friends? (A formal definition of construct validity is given below in the excerpt.)

See Appendix A to review the *mean, correlation coefficient*, and *statistical significance* before attempting this exercise.

Background Notes

The Comprehensive Receptive and Expressive Vocabulary Test (CREVT) is an individually administered test with two subtests: (1) *Receptive Vocabulary* in which the examiner says a series of words; for each word, the examinee selects from six pictures the one that best represents the word, and (2) *Expressive Vocabulary* in which the examiner says a series of words and asks the examinee to define each one. It was designed for use with examinees from ages 4 through 17.

Excerpt from the Manual

Construct validity, the final type of validity to be examined, relates to the degree to which the underlying traits of a test can be identified and the extent to which these traits reflect the theoretical model on which the test is based. Gronlund and Linn (1990) offered a three-step procedure for demonstrating this kind of validity. First, several constructs presumed to account for test performance are identified. Second, hypotheses are generated that are based on the identified constructs. Third, the hypotheses are verified by logical or empirical methods. Four basic constructs thought to underlie the CREVT and four related testable questions are discussed below. (*Editor's note*: Only three of the four questions are shown in this excerpt.)

1. Because vocabulary is developmental in nature, performance on the CREVT should be related strongly to chronological age.
2. Because the CREVT subtests both measure vocabulary (but in different ways), they should correlate highly with each other.
3. Because the CREVT measures vocabulary, its results should differentiate between groups of people known to be average and those known to be below average in vocabulary ability.

---

[1]Wallace, G. & Hammill, D. D. (1994). *Examiner's Manual: Comprehensive Receptive and Expressive Vocabulary Test*. Austin, TX: Pro-Ed. Copyright © 1994 by Pro-Ed. Reprinted with permission.

Age Differentiation

If vocabulary is indeed related to age, then one would expect the CREVT scores of the students in the normative sample to increase with age, which is precisely what happens. (See the mean CREVT raw scores achieved by the normative group found in Table 6.4.)[2] In addition, the correlation of the CREVT scores with the ages of the students in the normative sample is listed below; these coefficients are large and highly [statistically] significant ($p < .01$).

Receptive Vocabulary (Form A)	.72
Receptive Vocabulary (Form B)	.71
Expressive Vocabulary (Form A)	.69
Expressive Vocabulary (Form B)	.68

Table 6.4 *Mean Raw Scores*

	Receptive Vocabulary		Expressive Vocabulary	
	Form A	Form B	Form A	Form B
Age Interval	*M*	*M*	*M*	*M*
4	15	13	3	2
5	19	18	4	4
6	23	22	5	5
7	28	28	7	7
8	33	33	11	10
9	37	37	12	12
10	41	40	14	13
11	46	46	16	16
12	47	48	17	16
13	49	49	18	17
14	50	50	18	18
15	52	53	20	20
16	52	52	19	18
17	54	53	19	19

Interrelationship Among CREVT Values

The CREVT raw scores of the Receptive and Expressive Vocabulary subtests were correlated using the students in the normative sample as subjects. Age effects were partialled from each coefficient. The resulting coefficients are presented in Table 7.5. Applying MacEachron's (1982) rule of thumb interpretation for the size of Pearson *r*s to the coefficients in the table leads to the conclusion that the two CREVT subtests evidence a "high" relationship. This observation provides further support for CREVT's construct validity.

Table 7.5 *Correlation of Receptive and Expressive Vocabulary Subtests (decimals omitted)*

	Expressive Vocabulary (Form A)	Expressive Vocabulary (Form B)
Receptive Vocabulary (Form A)	77	79
Receptive Vocabulary (Form B)	76	77

---

[2]*Editor's note*: Only the relevant portions of Table 6.4 are reprinted in this excerpt.

Group Differentiation

Since a vocabulary test is supposed to identify those students with vocabulary problems, students identified as likely to have a higher than normal incidence of vocabulary problems should score relatively low on the CREVT. To test this hypothesis, the CREVT performance of 102 students in the normative sample who were classified as having disabilities was analyzed. Of these students, 32 were identified as having mental retardation, 33 were speech and language cases, and 37 had learning disabilities.

All three of these groups are known to evidence poor oral vocabulary ability relative to students who are not so classified. This being the case, one would expect the mean for these groups to be significantly lower than that of normal groups. In addition, one would predict that the sample with mental retardation would have the lowest CREVT scores, the speech and language cases would have the next lowest scores, and the group with learning disabilities would have, relatively speaking, the highest mean scores. In fact, this prediction was substantiated by the means and standard deviations reported in Table 7.6.

Table 7.6 *Means and Standard Deviations of Three Groups of Students with Disabilities*

Disability Group/CREVT Subtests	Mean	Standard Deviation
Mental Retardation		
Receptive Vocabulary (Form A)	67	6
Receptive Vocabulary (Form B)	67	7
Expressive Vocabulary (Form A)	62	10
Expressive Vocabulary (Form B)	62	10
Speech/Language		
Receptive Vocabulary (Form A)	83	9
Receptive Vocabulary (Form B)	83	9
Expressive Vocabulary (Form A)	82	10
Expressive Vocabulary (Form B)	82	7
Learning Disability		
Receptive Vocabulary (Form A)	89	12
Receptive Vocabulary (Form B)	88	12
Expressive Vocabulary (Form A)	90	11
Expressive Vocabulary (Form B)	87	11

Editor's note. Derived scores are shown in this table and, hence, are not directly comparable to the raw scores shown in Table 6.4.

Questions:

1. According to the excerpt, what is the second step in determining construct validity?

2. The correlation between age and CREVT scores is weakest for which subtest/form?

3. What is the difference between the mean raw score on Form A of Receptive Vocabulary at age 4 and at age 10?

4. Suppose the information under the heading *Age Differentiation* was the only information in the manual on the validity of the CREVT. In your opinion, would it be sufficient? Why? Why not?

5. The excerpt suggests that the correlations in Table 7.5 are "high." If you have a tests and measurements book, check to see whether your authors indicate what should be considered a "high" coefficient. Write your findings here.

6. In your opinion, how valuable is it to know that the scores on Expressive Vocabulary are correlated with scores on Receptive Vocabulary? Is this important information for judging the validity of the CREVT?

7. In your opinion, do the data support the third hypothesis? Explain.

8. On the whole, does the excerpt and the data presented in the excerpt convince you that the CREVT is a valid measure of vocabulary?

9. What other types of validity information would you like to see for the CREVT? Be specific.

10. The excerpt gives a brief definition of "construct validity." If you have a tests and measurements book, find the definition that your authors give. Does it match the one in the excerpt? Explain.

EXERCISE 11

Construct Validity: II

Gray Oral Reading Tests[1]

Guideline

See Exercise 10 to review the meaning of construct validity.

See Appendix A to review the *median* and *correlation coefficient* and *statistical significance* before attempting this exercise.

Background Notes

The Gray Oral Reading Tests–Third Edition (GORT-3) provides, among other things, (1) a Rate Score based on the time it takes an examinee to read passages orally, (2) an Accuracy Score based on the number of oral reading errors, (3) a Passage Score based on the combination of the previous two scores, and (4) a Comprehension Score based on an examinee's responses to multiple-choice items that are read aloud by an examiner.

The excerpt shown below covers one of seven sets of data relating to the construct validity of the GORT-3.

Excerpt from the Manual

Relationship to Other Language Scores

Since reading is only one aspect of a student's language ability, GORT-3 scores should correlate with other measures of language ability. This comparison was investigated in . . . separate studies. . . .

In the first study, GORT-3 performance on Form A was compared to the language scores on the CAT for 74 students (Grades 3 and 4) who were part of the normative sample. The correlation of these scores resulted in the coefficients reported in Table 4.10.

In the second study, 108 students (Grades 9 through 12) in the sample were given Form A of the GORT-3 and the Correctness of Expression and Literary Materials subtests of the ITED. The results of the correlational analysis are also reported in Table 4.10. Ninety-eight of these students had also taken Form B, and scores were also correlated with the ITED language scores and the results reported in Table 4.10.

In a third study, Form A of the GORT-3 was administered to 20 students attending a private elementary school in Austin, Texas. The students were also administered the Spelling subtest and the Written Language composite components of the DAB-2 and the Language and Writing subtests of the SCREEN. The standard scores of the GORT-3 and the language tests were intercorrelated, and the resulting coefficients corrected for attenuation and reported in Table 4.10.

In all, there are 65 coefficients reported in the table. All coefficients are significant at .05, and the median coefficient is .57 in magnitude. MacEachron (1982) classified a

[1]Wiederholt, J. L., & Bryant, B. R. (1992). *Examiner's Manual: Gray Oral Reading Tests–Third Edition.* Austin, TX: Pro-Ed. Copyright © 1992 by Pro-Ed. Reprinted with permission.

coefficient of this size as falling in the "moderate" range, providing further evidence of the construct validity of the GORT-3.

Table 4.10 *Correlation Between GORT-3 Scores and Language Tests (decimals omitted)*

Other Scores	Form A					Form B				
	RT	AC	PS	CS	ORQ	RT	AC	PS	CS	ORQ
CAT										
Spelling	55	46	53	45	60					
Mechanics	65	45	57	23	54					
Expression	72	59	68	49	73					
Total Language	73	53	70	37	67					
ITED										
Correctness of Expression	60	51	57	29	48	39	47	46	NS	30
Literary Materials	63	57	62	49	58	38	37	41	NS	37
DAB-2										
Spelling	63	76	71	28	53	72	67	71	41	60
Written Language	79	88	88	44	71	78	71	78	40	63
SCREEN										
Language	38	50	44	60	60					
Writing	NS	43	30	NS	26					

Note: RT = Rate; AC = Accuracy; PS = Passage Score; CS = Comprehension Score; ORQ = Oral Reading Quotient; CAT = *California Achievement Test;* ITED = *Iowa Tests of Educational Development;* DAB-2 = *Diagnostic Achievement Battery—Second Edition;* SCREEN = *Screening Children for Related Early Educational Needs.*

Questions:

1. The correlation coefficients for the CAT and GORT-3 in Table 4.10 are based on the performance of how many students?

2. The correlation coefficients for the SCREEN and GORT-3 in Table 4.10 are based on the performance of how many students?

3. What does "CS" stand for in Table 4.10?

4. What does "DAB-2" stand for in Table 4.10?

5. Decimals are omitted in Table 4.10. What is the value of the first correlation coefficient (55) *with the decimal*?

6. The GORT-3 Accuracy Scores have the weakest correlation with which CAT subtest?

7. The correlation coefficient for the relationship between the GORT-3 Accuracy Scores and the DAB-2 Written Language Scores is reported as 88. Would you characterize this as "strong," "moderate," or "weak"?

8. In light of the first sentence in the excerpt, it is reasonable to infer that the test makers expected to find a direct relationship between GORT-3 scores and spelling scores. Did they? Explain.

9. Which correlation coefficient reported in Table 4.10 indicates the weakest relationship?

10. What do you think "NS" means in Table 4.10?

11. According to the text in the excerpt, what is the value of the average coefficient in Table 4.10?

12. If the material in the excerpt were the only information on validity in the manual, would it be sufficient to convince you that the GORT-3 is a valid measure of reading?

13. In addition to information on the construct validity of a reading test, what other types of validity information would you like to have? Be specific.

Construct Validity: III

Beck Depression Inventory[1]

Guideline

To estimate construct validity, test makers sometimes correlate scores on a scale or test with scores on a number of other tests. When the pattern of correlations is consistent with what was expected, we can say that there is evidence of *convergent/discriminate validity*. For example, when the scores correlate more highly with a closely related scale (*convergent*) than with a less related scale (*discriminate*), we can interpret this as indicating validity. See Appendix A to review the *correlation coefficient* and *statistical significance* (as indicated by *p*) before attempting this exercise.

Background Notes

The Beck Depression Inventory–Second Edition (BDI-II) is a popular self-report inventory designed to measure the "severity of depression in adults and adolescents aged 13 years and older." The inventory covers content areas such as sadness, pessimism, loss of pleasure, self-dislike, and changes in appetite, tiredness or fatigue, suicidal thoughts, crying, and irritability.

Excerpt from the Manual

Table 3.4 shows the correlations between the BDI-II total scores and scores on several other psychological tests. These correlations are evidence of the convergent and discriminant validity of the BDI-II. The varying sample numbers shown in Table 3.4 are attributable to the use of different instruments by the four psychiatric clinics. With respect to the convergent validity of the BDI-II, the data indicate that the BDI-II is positively ($p <$ .001) related to both the Beck Hopelessness Scale (BHS; Beck & Steer, 1988) ($r = .68$) and the Scale for Suicide Ideation (SSI; Beck, Kovacs, & Weissman, 1979) ($r = .37$); the two psychological constructs measured by the BHS and the SSI have been described repeatedly as positively related to depression (Beck & Steer, 1987, 1988, 1991; Beck et al., 1988). The correlation between the Beck Anxiety Inventory (BAI; Beck & Steer, 1990) and the BDI-II scores was .60 ($p < .001$). Because depression and anxiety have been found to be correlated in clinical evaluations, this finding was not unexpected.

Further evidence of the convergent and discriminant validity of the BDI-II with respect to clinically rated depression and anxiety is also shown in Table 3.4. Of special importance is the finding that the BDI-II was more positively correlated ($r = .71$) with the Hamilton Psychiatric Rating Scale for Depression (HRSD; Hamilton, 1960)...than it was with the Hamilton Rating Scale for Anxiety (HARS; Hamilton, 1959) ... ($r = .47, ... p <$

---

[1]Beck, A. T., Steer, R. A., Brown, G. K. (1996). *Manual from the Beck Depression Inventory–Second Edition*. San Antonio: The Psychological Corporation. Copyright © 1996 by Aaron T. Beck. Reproduced by permission of the publisher, The Psychological Corporation. All rights reserved. "Beck Depression Inventory" and "BDI" are registered trademarks of The Psychological Corporation.

.01). The correlation between the HRSD-R and HARS-R was .51 ($p < .001$). These findings indicate a robust discriminant validity between depression and anxiety.

Table 3.4   Correlations Between BDI-II and Selected Scales

Scale	r
BHS ($N = 158$)	.68
SSI ($N = 158$)	.37
BAI ($N = 297$)	.60
HRSD-R ($N = 87$)	.71
HARS-R ($N = 87$)	.47

Note: All of the correlations were significant beyond the .001 level, one-tailed test, even after a Bonferroni adjustment of alpha/5.
BHS = *Beck Hopelessness Scale*, SSI = *Scale for Suicide Ideation*, BAI = *Beck Anxiety Inventory*, HRSD-R = *Revised Hamilton Psychiatric Rating Scale for Depression*, HARS-R = *Revised Hamilton Anxiety Rating Scale*

Questions:

1. The symbol *r* in the table stands for what?

2. What was the sample size for determining the relationship between the HRSD-R and the BDI-II?

3. Scores on the Beck Depression Inventory had the weakest relationship with scores on which other measure?

4. Scores on the Beck Depression Inventory had the strongest relationship with scores on which other measure?

5. Before reading the excerpt, would you have expected a strong relationship between depression and hopelessness? Did the test maker find a strong relationship? Explain.

6. Scores on the BDI-II were correlated with Hamilton's measures of depression and anxiety. Which one had a lower correlation with BDI-II scores? Does it make sense that this would be the one with the lower correlation?

7. The excerpt indicates that the data were collected at psychiatric clinics. In your opinion, does this limit the generalizability of the data to nonclinic populations? Explain.

8. The low values of p (such as $p < .001$) in the excerpt indicate that the correlation coefficients are larger than one would expect on the basis of chance alone (that is, they are statistically significant because there is a low probability that chance would create a correlation this large if, in truth, the two variables were unrelated). Does the fact that a correlation coefficient is statistically significant also indicate that the correlation is very strong? Explain.

9. In addition to the information reported in the excerpt, what other evidence of the validity of the BDI-II would you like to have?

EXERCISE 13

Percentile Ranks

Test of Pragmatic Language[1]

Guideline

A percentile rank indicates the percentage of a norm group who scored *equal to or lower than* an examinee.[2] Here's what Jennifer's percentile rank of 88 means: Jennifer's raw score (number of correct answers on the test) is as high or higher than the raw scores of 88 percent of the examinees in the norm group. (The norm group is often a national sample used to derive the percentile ranks.)

Background Notes

The Test of Pragmatic Language is an individually administered test that measures pragmatic language, which the test makers describe as "how language is used socially to achieve goals, and includes issues such as how communication is affected by different contexts and audiences, how messages are composed most effectively, and how different types of messages are put to best use." Among the groups for whom it is appropriate are examinees with learning disabilities, language disorders, reading impairments, and aphasia as well as students who are studying English as a second language.

Excerpt from the Manual

Percentiles, also called percentile scores or ranks, represent a value on a scale of 100 that indicates the percentage of the distribution that is equal to or below the value. Thus, a percentile rank of 75 for a child aged 11-6 [eleven years and six months] indicates that 75% of the standardization sample at that age scored at or below the raw score that converts to the 75th percentile. Percentile ranks are used often by educators and are easily understood.

Editors note: Portions of the table for converting raw scores to percentile ranks are shown on the next page in Table B.

---

[1]Phelps-Terasaki, D. & Phelps-Gunn, T. (1992). *Examiner's Manual: Test of Pragmatic Language.* Austin, TX: Pro-Ed, Inc. Copyright © 1992 by Pro-Ed. Reprinted with permission.
[2]For some tests, percentile ranks are derived in such a way that they indicate only the percentage of the norm group that scored below a given raw score.

Table B *Percentile Ranks for the TOPL*

Number of items passed	Chronological Age		
	5-0 to 5-5	5-6 to 5-11	6-0 to 6-5
0			
1			
2			
3			
4			
5			
6			
7	<0.3		
8	0.3	<0.3	
9	0.5	0.3	<0.3
10	1.0	0.4	0.3
11	2.0	0.5	0.4
12	3.0	1.0	0.6
13	4.0	2.0	1.0
14	5.0	3.0	2.0
15	9.0	4.0	3.0
16	12.0	5.0	4.0
17	17.0	8.0	5.0
18	23.0	11.0	6.0
19	31.0	15.0	9.0
20	38.0	21.0	12.0
21	46.0	27.0	17.0
22	50.0	35.0	23.0
23	55.0	42.0	31.0
24	62.0	50.0	38.0
25	71.0	57.0	46.0
26	77.0	62.0	50.0
27	81.0	71.0	60.0
28	84.0	77.0	69.0
29	89.0	81.0	73.0
30	92.0	86.0	79.0
31	95.0	90.0	83.0
32	96.0	93.0	84.0
33	98.0	96.0	89.0
34	>98.0	97.0	92.0
35		98.0	95.0
36		>98.0	96.0
37			98.0
38			>98.0
39			

Questions:

1. The top row of the table gives chronological ages. What does 5-11 mean?

2. A child who is 5-2 passed 17 items. What is his or her percentile rank?

3. A child who is 5-8 passed 17 items. What is his or her percentile rank?

4. A child who is 6-3 passed 17 items. What is his or her percentile rank?

5. If your answers to questions 2, 3 and 4 are correct, three children who passed 17 items have different percentile ranks. Explain why they are different.

6. A child who is between 5-0 and 5-5 passed 32 items. What percentage of the norm group at this age level scored at or below this child's raw score?

7. Explain the meaning of this symbol: >

8. Explain the meaning of this symbol: <

9. Consider two children in the 5-0 to 5-5 age group. One child passed 20 items and the other passed 21 items. In terms of percentile ranks, how many points separate the two children?

10. Consider two children in the 5-0 to 5-5 age group. One child passed 31 items and the other passed 32 items. In terms of percentile ranks, how many points separate the two children?

11. Consider your answers to questions 9 and 10. Speculate on why a 1-point difference in raw scores leads to a larger difference in percentile ranks at some points in the distribution than at other points.

EXERCISE 14

Stanines

Flanagan Aptitude Classification Test[1]

Guideline

Stanines are standardized scores expressed on a 9-point scale. Their meaning is described below in the excerpt. A raw score is the number of points earned on a test.

Background Notes

The Flanagan Aptitude Classification Test (FACT) consists of 16 separate aptitude tests (one for each of 16 job elements identified by studying critical behaviors in various jobs). The author suggests that the tests are useful for predicting success in various occupational and educational fields. Eight of the tests are mentioned in the excerpt. They are: *Inspection* (spotting flaws in a series of items), *Coding* (coding typical office information), *Memory* (remembering codes used in the Coding Test), *Scales* (reading technical scales, graphs and charts), *Arithmetic* (adding, subtracting, dividing and multiplying), *Patterns* (reproducing pattern outlines), *Tables* (reading numeric and alphanumeric tables), and *Mechanics* (understanding mechanical principles and mechanical movements).

Excerpt from the Manual

The stanine score is a standard score on a 9-point scale. A median stanine score of 5 on each of the tests represents average performance. Table 16 shows the meaning of each of the nine stanine scores. Tables 17 and 18 show the raw score to the stanine score conversion for educational samples. (*Editor's Note:* Only Tables 16 and 18 are shown in this excerpt.)

Table 16 *Meaning of Stanine Scores*

	Stanine								
	1	2	3	4	5	6	7	8	9
Description of the score	Very low	Low	Below average	A little below average	Average	A little above average	Above average	High	Very high
% of population receiving a lower score	2%	8%	17%	32%	50%	68%	83%	92%	98%

[1]Flanagan, J. C. (1994). *Examiner's Manual: Flanagan Aptitude Classification Test.* Copyright © 1994 by McGraw-Hill/London House. Reprinted with permission.

Table 18 *Raw Score to Stanine Conversions*

FACT	Stanine								
	1	2	3	4	5	6	7	8	9
1. Inspection	≤52	53-58	59-63	64-69	70-75	76-80	81-85	86-91	≥92
2. Coding	≤64	65-75	76-89	90-101	102-120	121-134	135-143	144-147	≥148
3. Memory	≤2	3-4	5-7	8-11	12-15	16-20	21-23	24-27	≥28
6. Scales	–	≤2	3-6	7-11	12-17	18-23	24-30	31-34	≥35
9. Arithmetic	≤12	13-23	24-33	34-43	44-54	55-63	64-71	72-78	≥79
10. Patterns	≤4	5-8	9-12	13-17	18-23	24-30	31-36	37-42	≥43
12. Tables	≤27	28-39	40-49	50-57	58-64	65-71	72-78	79-85	≥86
13. Mechanics	≤4	5	6-7	8	9-10	11-14	15-17	18-20	≥21

Questions:

1. What description is associated with a stanine of 7?

2. What description is associated with a stanine of 1?

3. What percentage of the population receives a stanine lower than 7?

4. What percentage of the population receives a stanine lower than 3?

5. Explain the meaning of this symbol: ≤

6. Explain the meaning of this symbol: ≥

7. An examinee who has a raw score of 11 on the Arithmetic Test has what stanine?

8. An examinee who has a raw score of 14 on the Memory Test has what stanine?

9. What score description is associated with the stanine that corresponds to a raw score of 9 on the Memory Test? (Hint: Look up the stanine in Table 18; then look up the description in Table 16.)

10. What score description is associated with the stanine that corresponds to a raw score of 119 on the Coding Test?

11. In terms of stanines, is a raw score of 60 on Inspection higher *or* lower than a raw score of 60 on Coding?

12. In terms of stanines, is a raw score of 40 on Patterns higher *or* lower than a raw score of 40 on Arithmetic?

13. For understanding how well an examinee performed on a test, are raw scores or stanines more helpful? Explain your answer.

14. When using stanines instead of raw scores, we are losing some information about differences among examinees. For example, all examinees with raw scores from 102 to 120 on Coding have a stanine of 5. Is this loss of information important? Explain.

IQ Scores

Wechsler Intelligence Scale for Children[1]

Guideline

IQ scores are standardized scores with a mean of 100 and a standard deviation of 15. They are more fully described below in the excerpt. See the Guideline for Exercise 13 to review percentile ranks, which are also mentioned in the excerpt.

In the Excerpt below, the authors indicate that two-thirds of examinees in a normal distribution fall within one standard deviation of the mean. A closer approximation is 68%.

See Appendix A to review the *mean* and *standard deviation* before attempting this exercise.

Background Notes

See Exercise 7 for background information on the Wechsler Intelligence Scale for Children–Third Edition.

Excerpt from the Manual

Each of the distributions of the Verbal, Performance, and Full Scale IQ scores…has a mean of 100 and a standard deviation (*SD*) of 15. A score of 100 on any of the three scales defines the performance of the average child of a given age on that scale. Scores of 85 and 115 correspond to 1 *SD* below and above the mean, respectively, whereas scores of 70 and 130 are 2 *SD*s from the mean. About two-thirds of all children obtain scores between 85 and 115, about 95% score in the 70–130 range, and nearly all obtain scores between 55 and 145 (3 *SD*s on either side of the mean).

Table 2.7 facilitates the interpretation of IQ…scores in terms of standard deviations and percentile ranks. The table is based on theoretical values for a normal distribution. The distributions of IQ and index scores obtained by the children in the standardization sample closely approximate these theoretical values.

Editor's note: Table 2.7 is shown on the next page.

See pg 47

Table 2.7   *Relation of IQ...Scores to Standard Deviations from the Mean and*
            Percentile Rank Equivalents

IQ Score	Number of *SD*s from the Mean	Percentile Rank Equivalent
145	+3	99.9
140	+2 2/3	99.6
135	+2 1/3	99
130	+2	98
125	+1 2/3	95
120	+1 1/3	91
115	+1	84
110	+2/3	75
105	+1/3	63
100	0 (Mean)	50
95	−1/3	37
90	−2/3	25
85	−1	16
80	−1 1/3	9
75	−1 2/3	5
70	−2	2
65	−2 1/3	1
60	−2 2/3	0.4
55	−3	0.1

Note: The percentile ranks are theoretical values for a normal distribution.

Questions:

1. What fraction of all children have IQs between 85 and 115?

2. What percentage of all children have IQs between 70 and 130?

3. A child with an IQ of 125 is how many standard deviations above the mean of 100?

4. A child who is zero standard deviations from the mean has what IQ score?

5. A child who has a percentile rank of 50 has what IQ score?

6. In terms of percentile ranks, is there much difference between a child with an IQ of 140 and a child with an IQ of 145? Explain.

7. A child who is one standard deviation above the mean has what percentile rank?

8. A child who has a percentile rank of 5 scored as high as or higher than what percentage of the children in the normal distribution?

9. If you had a child who scored two standard deviations below the mean, would this be a cause for concern to you? Explain.

10. In your opinion, would it be easier for a parent with no training in tests and measurements to understand their child's IQ score *or* their child's percentile rank? Explain.

11. What do you think a "standardization sample" is?

EXERCISE 16

Derived Scores and the Normal Curve

Peabody Picture Vocabulary Test[1]

Guideline

A *z*-score indicates how many standard deviation units an examinee is from the mean of the group. For example, if an examinee has a *z*-score of –1.00, he or she is one standard deviation below the mean. See the guidelines in Exercises 13 and 14 to review the meanings of percentile ranks and stanines. Note that the standard scores in this excerpt are expressed on the same scale as IQ scores. See Exercise 15 to review the meaning of IQ scores.

See Appendix A to review the *mean* and *standard deviation* before attempting this exercise.

Background Notes

The Peabody Picture Vocabulary Test–III (PPVT-III) is an individually adminis-tered, norm-referenced, wide-range test of hearing vocabulary, available in two parallel forms. Each form in this revision contains 175 test items. Each item has four simple black-and-white illustrations arranged in a multiple-choice format. The examinee's task is to select the picture considered to illustrate best the meaning of a stimulus word presented orally by the examiner. The PPVT-III was standardized on a national sample.

The Excerpt on the next page consists only of a figure that shows the different types of derived scores and their relationship with each other when the distribution of raw scores is normal, or has been normalized as in the case of the PPVT–III.

---

[1]*Peabody Picture Vocabulary Test–III* (1997). The excerpt is from the *Examiner's Manual* for the *PPVT–Revised* by Lloyd M. Dunn and Leota M. Dunn, published by American Guidance Service, Inc., 4201 Woodland Road, Circle Pines, MN 55014-1796. Copyright © 1981. Reproduced with permission of the author/publisher. All rights reserved.

Excerpt from the Manual

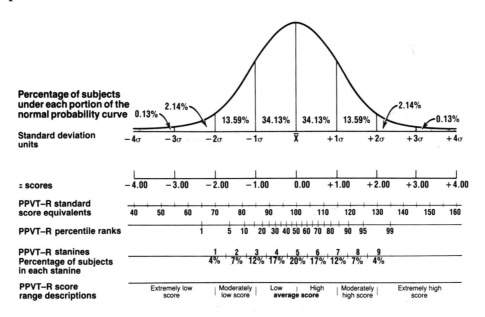

Figure 1.3 Interchangeability of different types of deviation-type norms when the distribution of raw scores is normal, or has been normalized as in the case of the PPVT–R.

Questions:

Note: The questions refer to the scores in the *normal distribution* shown in the excerpt.

1. What percentage of examinees scored below the mean?

    50%

2. What percentage of examinees scored between the mean and one standard deviation above the mean?   34.13%

3. What percentage of examinees scored more than three standard deviations above the mean?

    0.13%

4. A percentile rank of 50 corresponds to what standard score equivalent?

    100

5. Examinees with standard score equivalents of 130, 140, 150, and 160 all have what stanine?

6. An examinee with a z-score of 3.25 has what percentile rank?

    between 99 – 100

47

7. What percentage of examinees have a stanine of 1?

8. What is the score range description for a percentile rank of 93?

Moderately high Score

9. What is the score range description for a stanine of 9?

10. If you were using this test to award a scholarship to the highest scoring student on this test, would stanines be a good choice as the type of score to use? Explain.

NO

11. In your opinion, which of the types of scores in the excerpt would be most understandable to a parent who has not studied tests and measurements? Explain.

Percentile and/or descriptions

12. Speculate on why psychologists and educators rarely report z-scores to examinees.

They wont Get it

EXERCISE 17

Grade Equivalents

KeyMath[1]

Guideline

The manuals for many achievement tests provide norms tables that allow the test administrator to look up the number of correct answers (i.e., raw score) and convert it to a grade equivalent. The derivation of these scores and problems associated with them are described in the excerpt.

Background Notes

KeyMath–Revised (KeyMath-R) is an individually administered diagnostic mathematics test designed for use in the elementary grades and middle school. The subtests assess knowledge and skills in three areas: Basic Concepts (such as numeration and rational numbers), Operations (such as multiplication and division), and Applications (such as measurement, time and money, and problem solving).

Excerpt from the Manual

Grade equivalents. Grade-equivalent scores are frequently used in interpreting performance on academic achievement measures. They are provided for interpreting KeyMath-R total-test and area performance (Table 10). A grade equivalent indicates the grade in the standardization sample for which a given raw score was the average performance. For example, in Table 10 a grade equivalent of 8.0 corresponds to a total-test raw score of 193, which is the average total-test raw score for beginning eighth-graders. Grade equivalents for KeyMath-R range in tenths of a grade from K.0 (beginning kindergarten) to 9.9 (ninth grade, ninth month).

Grade equivalents must be interpreted with caution, particularly for students of very high or very low ability, or for students beyond the elementary grades. For example, it would be inappropriate to assume that a fifth-grader with a grade equivalent of 9.2 is truly functioning as a ninth-grader. Rather, he or she scored about the same on KeyMath-R as the average student in the second month of the ninth grade tested in the standardization sample. Undoubtedly, there are aspects of the middle school curriculum of which the fifth-grader is totally unaware. Similarly, a fifth-grader with a grade equivalent of 2.8 knows many things beyond the knowledge of an average student in the eighth month of grade 2. These difficulties are compounded at the middle school and secondary levels, where the variety of mathematics classes offered further separates student functioning.

[Table 10 is shown on the next page.]

Table 10   Grade Equivalents Corresponding to Area and Total-Test Raw Scores

Grade Equivalent	Basic Concepts	Operations	Applications	Total Test
		Raw Score		
Above 9.9	55–66	80–90	80–102	214–258
9.9	–	–	–	213
9.8	54	–	79	212
9.7	–	79	–	–
9.6	–	–	–	211
9.5	–	–	78	210
9.4	–	78	–	209
9.3	53	–	–	208
9.2	–	–	77	207
9.1	–	77	–	206
9.0	–	–	–	205
8.9	52	–	76	204
8.8	–	76	–	203
8.7	–	–	75	202
8.6	51	75	–	200–201
8.5	–	–	74	199
8.4	–	–	–	198
8.3	50	74	73	197
8.2	–	–	–	196
8.1	–	73	72	194–195
8.0	49	–	–	193
7.9	–	72	71	191–192
7.8	48	–	70	189–190
7.7	–	71	–	188
7.6	–	70	69	186–187
7.5	47	–	68	184–185
7.4	–	69	–	183
7.3	–	68	67	181–182
7.2	46	67	–	179–180
7.1	–	66	66	177–178
7.0	45	–	65	175–176
6.9	–	65	–	173–174
6.8	–	64	64	171–172
6.7	44	63	63	169–170
6.6	–	–	62	167–168
6.5	43	62	–	165–166
6.4	–	61	61	163–164

Note. Only a portion of the table is shown here.

Questions:

1. If a grade equivalent of 9.5 stands for "ninth grade, fifth month," for what does a grade equivalent of 7.0 stand?

2. In order to derive the grade equivalents for the Applications test, the test maker had to administer the test at various grade levels and determine the average raw score at each grade level. What was the average raw score on Applications at the beginning of grade seven?

3. If a student has a raw score of 50 on Basic Concepts, what is her grade equivalent score?

4. If a student has a Total Test raw score of 190, what is his grade equivalent score?

5. Suppose a student who is in the the sixth grade obtains a Total Test raw score of 205, which corresponds to a grade equivalent of 9.0. According to the excerpt, should we infer that she is functioning in math at the ninth-grade level? Would it be wise to assign her a ninth-grade math textbook? Explain.

6. Consider the last sentence in the excerpt. Then consider that in one school the students are required to take geometry in the ninth grade while in another school the students are required to take algebra in the ninth grade. Would grade equivalents be a good type of score to use to compare the achievement of the ninth-graders in the two schools? Explain.

7. Suppose you were teaching students in grade 7.0 and you administered the KeyMath-R Basic Concepts test to them and got an average raw score of 45 for your class, which corresponds to a grade equivalent of 7.0. However, as you examined the scores of individual students, you noticed that half the students had scores above 45 and half had scores below 45. Would it be fair to say that something is *seriously wrong* because half the students are below grade level, as indicated by grade equivalents? Explain.

8. Suppose at the beginning of a school year, a student earned a raw score of 76 on the Operations test and at the end of the year earned two more points for a raw score of 78 on this test. By how many grade equivalent months did this student's score increase?

9. Consider your answer to question 8. Does it make sense that a student who increased by only two raw score points would get such an increase in grade equivalents? Does there seem to be a problem here? Explain.

10. Consider another student who earned a raw score of 66 on the Operations test at the beginning of a school year and at the end of the year earned two more points for a raw score of 68 on this test (also an increase of 2 raw score points; see question 8). By how many grade equivalent months did this student's score increase? Compare your answer to this question to your answer to question 8. Does there seem to be a problem here?

EXERCISE 18

Age Equivalents

Vineland Adaptive Behavior Scales[1]

Guideline

Age equivalents are given in norms tables for some tests and scales. The tables allow the test administrator to look up the number of correct answers (i.e., raw score) and convert it to an age equivalent. The derivation of age equivalents and problems associated with interpreting them are described in the excerpt. The term *standardization sample* mentioned in the excerpt refers to a norm group on which the age equivalents were derived.

Background Notes

The Vineland Adaptive Behavior Scales assess personal and social efficiency of individuals from birth to adulthood. It covers the domains of Communication, Daily Living Skills, Socialization, and Motor Skills. Typically, an interviewer reads the items to a child's parents. The child's score is determined by the parents' responses.

Excerpt from the Manual

Age equivalents have long been used in educational and psychological testing. The mental age associated with intelligence tests and the "Social Age" obtained in the Vineland Social Maturity Scale are examples of age equivalents. The age equivalent represents the raw score that was the average performance of individuals of a given chronological age in the standardization sample. For example, an age equivalent of 7-10 (7 years 10 months) indicates that the raw score corresponding to the age equivalent was the average raw score for individuals aged 7 years 10 months in the standardization sample. Age equivalents are useful only when traits that show a clear and consistent increase in performance with age are being measured.

Age equivalents often are readily understandable to people who are unfamiliar with statistical concepts. They leave much to be desired, however, because the scale units are unequal. "One year's growth" has a very different meaning at different points in the age continuum and for different areas of adaptive behavior. In the Communication domain, performance increases more between the ages of 2 and 3 than between the ages of 10 and 11… Because of their limitations, age equivalents should be used sparingly, if at all, when reporting results. [Table B.10 shows part of the table for converting raw scores to age equivalents.]

Table B.10   Age Equivalents Corresponding to Domain Raw Scores (Partial Table)

	Communication	Daily Living Skills	Socialization	Motor Skills
Age Equivalent		Raw Score		
6-11	101	118	91	–
6-10	100	117	–	–
6-9	–	116	90	–
6-8	99	115	–	–
6-7	98	114	89	–
6-6	97	113	–	–
6-5	–	–	88	–
6-4	96	112	–	–
6-3	95	111	87	–
6-2	94	110	–	–
6-1	–	109	86	–
6-0	93	107-108	85	–
5-11	92	106	84	70+[a]
5-10	91	105	–	–
5-9	–	103-104	83	69
5-8	90	102	82	–
5-7	89	101	81	–
5-6	88	100	80	–
5-5	87	98-99	79	68
5-4	–	97	–	–
5-3	86	96	78	67
5-2	85	94-95	77	–
5-1	84	93	76	66
5-0	83	92	–	–

[a] For Motor Skills domain raw scores of 70, 71, and 72, record an age equivalent of "above 5-11."

Questions:

1. In addition to this type of scale (i.e., adaptive behavior scale), what other type of scale or test is mentioned as being associated with age equivalents?

2. Thinking about human development, do you agree with the authors that communication skills usually increase more between ages 2 and 3 than between ages 10 and 11?

3. According to the excerpt, should age equivalents be used frequently?

4. What age equivalent corresponds to a raw score of 93 on Daily Living Skills?

5. If a child has a raw score of 71 on Motor Skills, what is his or her age equivalent?

6. Suppose a child was tested and received a raw score of 79 on Socialization. When she was tested again a year later, her raw score had increased 4 raw score points to 83. In terms of age equivalents, by how many months did her score increase?

7. Suppose another child was tested and received a raw score of 86 on Socialization. When he was tested again a year later, his raw score had increased 4 raw score points to 90. In terms of age equivalents, by how many months did his score increase?

8. Consider your answers to questions 6 and 7. Notice that both children increased 4 raw score points on Socialization, but their age equivalents indicate that the second child had twice as much growth as the first one. Does this make sense? Is there something wrong here? Explain.

9. Consider the authors' statement that "Age equivalents are useful only when traits that show a clear and consistent increase in performance with age are being measured." In light of this, would age equivalents make sense for measuring knowledge of current events among middle-age adults? Explain.

10. What is your opinion of the authors' statement that "Age equivalents often are readily understandable to people who are unfamiliar with statistical concepts?" Given what you now know about age equivalents, do you think that they are easy to explain fully to people who are not familiar with statistical concepts? Explain.

11. Speculate on why test makers continue to offer norms tables allowing test users to convert raw scores to age equivalents despite their limitations and the authors' assertion that they should be used "sparingly."

EXERCISE 19

Norm Group Composition: I

The Adaptive Behavior Evaluation Scale[1]

Guideline

The norm group (also known as the "normative sample" or "standardization sample") is the group whose performance is used to derive scores such as percentile ranks and standard scores. For major tests, test makers use samples of examinees drawn from throughout the United States. The representativeness of the samples determines the meaningfulness of the derived scores. Information on the composition of norm groups usually can be found in test manuals.

Background Notes

The Adaptive Behavior Evaluation Scale–School Version is designed to help educators make diagnostic, placement, and programming decisions for mentally retarded and emotionally disturbed/behaviorally disordered children and adolescents. Raters (usually teachers) rate students on items in ten areas: Communication, Self-Care (e.g., toileting, dressing, grooming), Home Living, Social, Community Use (e.g., shopping, using public transportation), Self-Direction (scheduling and completing tasks), Health and Safety, Functional Academics (i.e., academic skills needed for independent living), Leisure, and Work.

Excerpt from the Manual

Data were collected for the normative sample from 7,124 individual students from 24 states, which covers the four major geographical regions of the United States. States participating in the data collection for standardization purposes were Arizona, Arkansas, California, Colorado, Georgia, Idaho, Illinois, Iowa, Kansas, Kentucky, Michigan, Minnesota, Missouri, New Jersey, New Mexico, Ohio, Oklahoma, Oregon, Pennsylvania, South Carolina, Tennessee, Texas, Vermont, and Wyoming. Responses from age groups for students under 5 years of age and over 18 years of age were less than adequate and subsequently dropped from the norming procedures. Demographic characteristics, sex, ethnic origin, residence, and parental occupation of the represented age groups are shown in Table 1.

Data represented as "Percentage of Nation" represent percentage from the *Statistical Abstract of the United States*, 1992. These characteristics are included in order to present the wide dispersion of norming participants through cultures, age groups, and backgrounds.

---

[1]McCarney, S. B. *The Adaptive Behavior Evaluation Scale–Revised.* Copyright © 1995 by Hawthorne Educational Services, Inc., 800 Gray Oak Drive, Columbia, MO 65201. 1-800-542-1673. Reprinted by permission.

Table 1 *Characteristics of Students in the Standardization Sample*

	Percent of Sample	Percent of Nation
Sex		
Male	50.4	48.8
Female	49.6	51.2
Race		
White	84.0	76.2
African American	8.8	11.3
Hispanic	3.2	8.7
American Indian	0.2	0.8
Other	3.7	3.0
Residence		
Urban/Suburban	56.8	75.2
Rural	43.2	24.8
Geographic Area		
Northeast	3.6	20.0
North Central	48.2	24.0
South	24.5	35.0
West	23.7	22.0
Father's Occupation		
White Collar	32.4	30.6
Blue Collar	36.7	40.9
Service	9.8	9.8
Farm	5.6	3.8
Other	15.6	15.0
Mother's Occupation		
White Collar	31.1	34.3
Blue Collar	20.4	17.3
Service	17.3	18.7
Farm	1.6	1.2
Other	29.5	28.6

Questions:

1. How many individuals were in the norm group?

2. How many states are represented by the norm group?

3. In your opinion, how important is it for all 50 states to be represented in a norm group?

4. Why were individuals under 5 years of age and over 18 years of age dropped from the norm group?

5. The excerpt uses the term "demographic characteristics." What do you think this term means?

6. In Table 1, "Percent of Nation" is based on information from which publication?

7. Which races are *overrepresented* in the sample (when compared with the percentages in the United States)?

8. What is your opinion of combining Urban and Suburban into one category?

9. Which father's occupation is *underrepresented* in the sample?

10. For which one characteristic is the percentage in the sample identical to the percentage in the nation?

11. Does it surprise you that most of the percentages in the sample are different from the percentages in the nation? Explain.

12. Based on the data in Table 1, what is your overall opinion on the representativeness of the sample?

Norm Group Composition: II

The Sixteen Personality Factor Questionnaire[1]

Guideline

See Exercise 19 for the guideline on norm groups.

The term *sample stratification* refers to drawing examinees separately from subgroups when sampling. For example, when test makers draw a sample of females separately from the sample of males, they are stratifying on the basis of gender. The purpose of stratifying on gender is to make sure that females and males in the sample are represented in the correct proportions. (Note that if test makers drew names out of a hat that contained both females and males without stratifying, they could end up with too many females or too many males in their norm group.)

See Appendix A to review the *mean* and *standard deviation* before attempting this exercise.

Background Notes

The Sixteen Personality Factor Questionnaire (16PF) is a self-report measure of 16 primary components of personality.

Excerpt from the Manual

Standardization

The final experimental form of the fifth edition was administered to a large group (N = 4,449), and then a stratified random sampling was used to create the final normative sample of 2,500. Sample stratification was done on the basis of gender, race, age, and educational variables, with the target number for each variable being derived from 1990 U.S. Census figures (Conn & Rieke, 1994a). Demographic details about the norm group are presented in Table 8, including the extent to which the sample matches the census figures. . . . The following summarizes the norm sample demographics:

1. Size of the norm sample is 2,500: 1,245 males and 1,255 females (49.8% male, 50.2% female).
2. Ages range from 15 to 92, with a mean age of 33.3 years.
3. Years of education completed range from 7 to 25, with a mean of 13.6 years (standard deviation of 3.30).
4. The sample is 80.4% Caucasian, 12.8% African American, 3.0% Asian American, 2.3% Native American, and 9.0% Hispanic. The Hispanic sample crosses racial groups, and for this reason, the total sample exceeds 100%.

---

[1]Russell, M. & Karol, D. (1994). *16PF ® Fifth Edition Administrator's Manual.* Copyright © 1994 by the Institute for Personality and Ability Testing, Inc. Reproduced with permission. "16PF" is a registered trademark belonging to the Institute for Personality and Ability Testing.

5. Approximately 16% of those in the sample reside in Northeastern states, 15% in Southeastern states, 28% in North Central states, 14% in South Central states, and 24% in Western states.

Table 8 *Norm Sample Demographics (N = 2500, 1245 Males, 1255 Females)*

GENDER		Number in Sample	Percent in Sample	Percent in 1990 Census
	Male	1245	49.8%	48.7%
	Female	1255	50.2%	51.3%

RACE		Number in Sample	Percent in Sample	Percent in 1990 Census
	African American	321	12.8%	12.1%
	Asian	76	3.0%	2.9%
	Caucasian	2010	80.4%	80.2%
	Native American	58	2.3%	1.0%
	Other	35	1.5%	3.8%
	Hispanic Origin	224	9.0%	9.0%

Note: Totals add up to over 100% since Hispanics also endorsed one of the five race categories

AGE GROUP	Respondents' Age (years)	Number in Sample	Percent in Sample	Percent in 1990 Census
	15 to 17	329	13.2%	4.6%
	18 to 24	415	16.6%	13.8%
	25 to 44	1216	48.6%	41.7%
	45 to 54	371	14.8%	12.9%
	55 to 64	116	4.6%	10.8%
	65 and over	53	2.2%	16.2%

EDUCATION LEVEL	Respondents' Education	Number in Sample	Percent in Sample	Percent in 1990 Census
	H.S. Grad or less	1107	44.3%	61.5%
	Some College	617	24.7%	22.7%
	College Graduate	776	31.0%	15.8%

Questions:

1. What determined the target number for each variable?

2. What was the average age of examinees in the norm group?

3. What is the standard deviation of the number of years of education completed?

4. Are males *or* females slightly overrepresented in the sample (when compared with Census data)?

5. Why do the percentages for race of examinees sum to more than 100%?

6. In your opinion, is the norm group sample reasonably representative in terms of race? Explain.

7. Which age group in the norm group sample is the most underrepresented?

8. Which educational level group in the norm group sample is the most over-represented?

9. Is it possible to determine from the excerpt whether the norm group sample is representative in terms of their geographic distribution? Explain.

10. Only 2,500 of the 4,449 tested were used in the norm group (i.e., normative sample). Speculate on why the test makers did not use all 4,449.

11. Are there other demographic variables that the test makers might have considered? Explain.

12. What is your overall opinion on the representativeness of the norm group sample?

13. In your opinion, how important is the type of information presented in the excerpt for those who will be interpreting scores? Explain.

EXERCISE 21

Standard Error of Measurement: I

Peabody Picture Vocabulary Test[1]

Guideline

A standard error of measurement (SEM) is a "margin of error" used to interpret a score. If you add the standard error of measurement to an examinee's score and then subtract it from the score, you obtain the limits of the 68% confidence interval; that is, you obtain the points between which we have 68% confidence that an examinee's true score lies. More information on the interpretation of the SEM is provided in the excerpt.

Background Notes

See Exercise 16 for background information on the Peabody Picture Vocabulary Test (PPVT).

Excerpt from the Manual

The true score is never known because some degree of measurement error is always present in the obtained score. Measurement errors occur because all human behavior varies from time to time, and because all psychometric measuring devices are imprecise to some degree. The standard error of measurement (SEM) is the statistic used to take into account the effects of error in the interpretation of individual test scores.

The SEM is added to, and subtracted from, the obtained score to define a confidence band around the obtained score. . . . The chances are about 68 in 100 (or about 2 out of 3) that the true score will not differ from the obtained score by as much as ± 1 SEM, and about 95 in 100 that the true score will not differ from the obtained score by as much as ± 2 SEM. Nevertheless, it is very important to note that the chances are greatest that the true score closely approximates the obtained score. Therefore, *the obtained score is the best single estimate of the true score.*

Table 1.1 lists the PPVT–R standard errors of measurement (rounded to the nearest whole numbers) for both raw scores and standard score equivalents, by age group, for Form L and Form M. The median standard error of measurement for raw scores is 6 points overall, and 5 points for adults. *For standard score equivalents, the median value is 7 points for all ages.* These median values provide good overall estimates of the PPVT standard errors of measurement. However, some users may wish to use the more precise values for each age group, given in Table 1.1.

Table 1.1 *PPVT–R Standard Errors of Measurement for Raw Scores and Standard Score Equivalents, by Age Group, for Form L and Form M*

| Age Group* | Standard Error of Measurement | | | |
| | For Raw Scores | | For Standard Score Equivalents | |
	Form L	Form M	Form L	Form M
2-6–2-11	4	4	6	7
3-0–3-5	5	6	7	8
3-6–3-11	6	6	7	7
4-0–4-5	7	7	7	7
4-6–4-11	7	7	8	7
5-0–5-5	6	7	7	8
5-6–5-11	5	7	5	7
6-0–6-5	7	6	8	7
6-6–6-11	6	6	7	7
7-0–7-11	6	4	7	5
8-0–8-11	7	6	9	7
9-0–9-11	6	5	7	6
10-0–10-11	6	6	6	7
11-0–11-11	4	5	5	6
12-0–12-11	6	6	6	7
13-0–13-11	6	6	6	6
14-0–14-11	6	5	7	5
15-0–15-11	8	6	8	6
16-0–16-11	5	5	6	6
17-0–17-11	7	7	8	8
18-0–18-11	8	7	9	7
19-0–24-11	5	5	6	6
25-0–29-11	5	5	7	7
30-0–34-11	5	5	7	7
35-0–40-11	5	5	6	6
Median	6	6	7	7

*Note: Age groups are reported in years and months; for example, 2-6–2-11 represents 2 years, 6 months through 2 years, 11 months.

Questions:

1. Explain the meaning of "7-0–7-11" in the table.

2. What is the value of the SEM for the raw score on Form M for someone who is 18 years and 8 months old?

3. Consider an examinee who is 8½ years old who has taken Form M of the test and earned a standard score of 110. What are the limits of the 68% confidence interval for the examinee's standard score? (Use the more precise value of the SEM in the body of the table—not the average or overall value.)

4. For the examinee described in question 3, what are the limits of the 95% confidence interval for the examinee's standard score? (Use the more precise value of the SEM in the body of the table—not the average or overall value.)

5. If your answers to questions 3 and 4 are correct, the confidence interval for question 4 is larger than the interval for question 5. Does this make sense? Explain.

6. The last row of the table shows the "median" values of the SEM. What is the median?

7. Consider an examinee who is 6 years and 2 months old who has taken Form L of the test and earned a standard score of 97. What are the limits of the 68% confidence interval for the examinee's standard score? (Use the median value of the SEM for all ages given in the text of the excerpt.)

8. The average standard score on the PPVT-R is 100 (see the figure in Exercise 16). Consider the examinee in question 3. Can we say with 68% confidence that the examinee is above the average of 100? Explain.

9. Suppose you were reporting the confidence interval for the examinee in question 7 to his or her parents. Assume that the parents had no training in tests and measurements. How would you explain the meaning of the interval (in your own words)?

10. In your opinion, is it better to report the obtained score or a confidence interval when reporting the results to parents? Why?

11. Suppose someone foolishly administered the Peabody Picture Vocabulary Test in English to a child who was proficient in Spanish but not in English. Clearly, there may be a large error in the score because of bias. Will the SEM help take account of this bias? Explain. (Note: You may need to review the rationale for the SEM in your textbook before answering this question.)

EXERCISE 22

Standard Error of Measurement: II

Behavior Dimensions Scale–School Version[1]

Guideline

See Exercise 21 to review the meaning of the standard error of measurement.

Background Notes

The Behavior Dimensions Scale–School Version measures Attention-Deficit Hyperactivity Disorder, Oppositional Defiant Disorder, Conduct Disorder, Avoidant Personality Disorder, Generalized Anxiety Disorder, and Major Depressive Episode. Teachers use the scale to rate students. The scale refers to overt behaviors; teachers rate frequency of the behaviors. Teachers are not asked to make assumptions or draw conclusions in their ratings.

Excerpt from the Manual

Table 7 presents the standard errors of measurement for each age-sex group for the subscales of the Behavior Dimensions Scale–School Version. The figures represent the confidence level around the *raw* score for each subscale. There is a 68 percent chance that a child/youth's true score lies within one standard error on either side of his measured score; an 80 percent chance that it lies within 1.28 standard errors; a 95 percent chance that it lies within two standard errors; and a 99 percent chance that it lies within three standard errors.

For example, consider a 9-year-old boy with a Hyperactive-Impulsive raw score of 40. . . . There is a 95 percent chance that his true abilities lie in a range represented by raw scores between 32.96 and 47.04...

Table 7 *Standard Errors of Measurement*

	Inatten-tive	Hyper-active Impul-sive	Oppo-sitional Defiant	Conduct	Avoid-ant Person-ality	Anxiety	Depress-ion	Total
Males, 5 years	2.76	4.08	3.22	2.07	1.65	2.54	3.26	9.48
Males, 6-7 years	2.30	3.55	2.62	1.76	1.51	2.20	2.90	8.33
Males, 8 years	2.46	3.51	2.77	1.82	1.86	2.38	3.19	8.99
Males, 9-10 years	2.35	3.52	2.63	1.68	1.65	2.28	3.16	8.55
Males, 11-12 years	2.15	3.40	2.63	1.74	1.67	2.17	3.09	7.98
Males, 13-15 years	2.21	3.41	2.91	2.08	2.08	2.32	3.48	8.85
Females, 5 years	2.10	3.13	2.38	1.58	1.53	2.02	1.67	7.62
Females, 6 years	1.93	2.95	1.75	1.06	0.94	1.78	2.03	6.36

This table is continued on the next page.

[1]McCarney, S. B (1995). *The Behavior Dimensions Scale.* Copyright © 1995 by Hawthorne Educational Services, Inc., 800 Gray Oak Drive, Columbia, MO 65201; 1-800-542-1673. Reprinted with permission.

Table 7 *Continued*

	Inatten-tive	Hyper-active Impul-sive	Oppo-sitional Defiant	Conduct	Avoid-ant Person-ality	Anxiety	Depress-ion	Total
Females, 7-8 years	1.94	3.01	1.99	1.28	1.20	1.80	2.42	6.58
Females, 9 years	2.07	2.76	2.68	1.37	1.34	1.77	2.51	6.54
Females, 10-12 years	1.71	2.38	1.68	1.14	1.28	1.47	2.18	5.66
Females, 13-15 years	1.65	2.75	2.22	1.75	1.70	1.70	2.71	6.55
All subjects	2.10	3.13	2.38	1.58	1.53	2.02	1.67	7.62

Questions:

1. The excerpt mentions the term "true score." If you have a tests and measurements book, look up the term and write its definition here.

2. The standard error of measurement for Conduct is lowest for which age/sex group?

3. What is the standard error of measurement for a 5-year-old female on Anxiety?

4. If the female in question 3 has a raw score of 34 on Anxiety, there is a 68% chance that her true score lies between what two values?

5. For the female in questions 3 and 4 , there is a 95% chance that her true score lies between what two values?

6. In questions 4 and 5, you computed what are known as "confidence intervals" for estimating the true score. If your work is correct, the 95% confidence interval is wider than the 68% confidence interval. Does this make sense? Explain.

7. A 5-year-old male has a raw score of 45 on Hyperactive/Impulsive. There is an 80% chance that his true score lies between what two values?

8. No test has perfect validity and reliability when tried out with large groups. If you have a tests and measurements book, examine it to find out if the standard error of measurement takes into account errors due to less than perfect reliability *or* less than perfect validity. Write your findings here.

Standard Error of Measurement and Alternate-Forms Reliability

Stanford Achievement Test Series[1]

Guideline

To review the standard error of measurement, see the Guideline for Exercise 21. Additional information on its meaning and interpretation are given below in the excerpt. Standard errors of measurement are based, in part, on the reliability estimates for tests. In the excerpt shown below, *alternate-forms* reliability was used. This type of reliability can be obtained only when there are two alternate forms of a test (that is, the same skills are tested with two forms that contain somewhat different content). To get the reliability coefficient, one group of students takes both forms (usually at different times) and then the two sets of scores are correlated. Note that when a correlation coefficient is used for this purpose, it is called an alternate-forms reliability coefficient. See Appendix A to review the *correlation coefficient* before attempting this exercise.

Background Notes

First published in 1923, the Stanford Achievement Test Series has been a popular achievement test battery. It is now in its ninth edition; hence it is often referred to as the "Stanford 9." It "measures students' school achievement in reading, language arts, mathematics, science, and social science."

Excerpt from the Manual

Standard errors of measurement give information regarding the degree to which chance fluctuations in test scores can be expected. For example a standard error of 3.0 raw score units means that chance fluctuations within 3 points of an obtained score can be expected about two-thirds of the time.

An important estimate of reliability is *alternate-forms* reliability. This is a rigorous measure of test precision since it takes into account differences arising from different testing situations and from different but equivalent test content. Alternate-forms reliability coefficients, standard errors of measurement, and related data for the multiple-choice battery are presented in [the table on the next page.]

---

[1]From the Technical Data Manual for the Stanford Achievement Test: Ninth Edition. Copyright © 1996 by Harcourt Brace & Company. Reprinted by permission. All rights reserved.

Table G-3   Alternate-Forms Reliability Coefficients, Standard Errors of Measurement, and Related Data for the Primary 3 Equating of Forms Sample* (*Partial Table*)

Subtest/Total	Number of Items	N	Form S			Form T			r
			Mean	S.D.	SE_m	Mean	S.D.	SE_m	
Total Reading	84	605	57.0	14.4	4.7	57.2	15.2	4.9	0.89
Reading Vocabulary	30	605	22.0	5.1	2.2	21.8	5.4	2.4	0.80
Reading Comprehension	54	605	35.0	10.0	3.9	35.4	10.6	4.1	0.85
Total Mathematics	76	639	51.9	12.4	4.0	51.3	12.2	3.9	0.90
Problem Solving	46	639	31.5	7.4	3.0	31.0	7.1	2.9	0.84
Procedures	30	639	20.4	6.0	2.6	20.2	5.9	2.5	0.82

*In terms of raw scores.

Questions:

1. Which subtest/total test has the highest alternate-forms reliability?

2. Which subtest/total test has the lowest alternate-forms reliability?

3. The standard error of measurement for the Total Mathematics score is based on the performance of how many examinees?

4. Which subtest/total test on Form S has the smallest standard error of measurement?

5. Suppose Sylvester obtained a Total Reading raw score of 55 on Form T. If he took this test repeatedly (in theory), his raw score would probably fluctuate between what two score values (two-thirds of the time)? (Hint: Subtract the standard error of measurement from his raw score, and then add it to his raw score to get the two values. These values are called the *limits of the 68% confidence interval* for his score.)

6. Evaluate Sylvester's score in relation to the mean of the sample on which Table G-3 is based. Do the limits of the 68% confidence interval for his Total Reading raw score include the mean value for the sample?

7. Suppose Jennifer obtained a Total Reading raw score of 60 on Form T. What are the limits of the 68% confidence interval for her score?

8. Consider Jennifer's 68% confidence interval on Total Reading on Form T. Would you be willing to say that she is truly superior to the average person in the sample (with a mean of 57.2)?

9. Do the 68% confidence intervals for Sylvester and Jennifer overlap (i.e., are some of the possible scores for Sylvester also possible scores for Jennifer)?

10. Suppose Melissa obtained a raw score of 59 on Total Mathematics (Form S). What are the limits of the 68% confidence interval for her score?

11. To get a confidence interval in which we can have about 95% confidence, we can double the value of the standard error of measurement before adding it and subtracting it from an examinee's score. Use this information to compute the limits of the 95% confidence interval for Melissa's Total Mathematics raw score.

12. Does Melissa's 95% confidence interval include the sample's mean of 51.9? Are you willing to conclude that she is truly superior to the average person in the sample? Explain.

13. Theory tells us that tests with more items tend to be more reliable. Do the statistics in the table support this? Explain.

Significance of Intra-Ability Difference Scores

Gray Oral Reading Tests[1]

Guideline

When interpreting scores, examiners are often interested in determining an examinee's areas of strengths and weaknesses. For example, an examinee might have a higher score in math computations than in math word problems. We might want to know if this examinee's computations score is *significantly* higher than the word problems score. Test manuals often provide guidance on how to determine this, as illustrated in the excerpt below.

See Appendix A to review *statistical significance* before attempting this exercise.

Background Notes

See the Background Notes for Exercise 11 for background information on the Gray Oral Reading Tests–Third Edition (GORT-3). The standard scores for each of the subtests have a mean of 10 and a standard deviation of 3.

Excerpt from the Manual

Conducting Intra-Ability Discrepancy Analyses

Clinically useful information can be obtained by examining a person's reading strengths and weaknesses. To conduct an intra-ability analysis of strengths and weaknesses, Difference Scores (i.e., mathematical differences between two test scores) are calculated. Difference Scores can be computed . . . between selected GORT-3 subtests.

When comparing test scores, the fundamental question is, How discrepant must two test scores be for the difference to be significant? Reynolds (1985) offers a regression procedure for determining how large a Difference Score must be to obtain statistical significance. This formula can be used if the intercorrelation between two scores is known and if reliability coefficients for both scores are available. Because both indices are available with respect to the GORT-3 subtests, we were able to use Reynolds's procedure to generate Table 3.2, which provides minimum Difference Scores for comparing GORT-3 subtests.

Note that comparisons cannot be made between Rate and the Passage Score nor between Accuracy and the Passage Score. The reason for this is quite simple: Both Rate and Accuracy contribute to the Passage Score, rendering comparisons meaningless.

To use the table, compute a Difference Score by subtracting the lower score from the higher score. Consult the appropriate table to see if the score is significant. As an example, consider Jonathan's standard score performance on Form A of Rate (9) and Accuracy (4). His Difference Score is 5 points. Looking at Table 3.2, we see that the

---

[1]Wiederholt, J. L., & Bryant, B. R.(1992). *Examiner's Manual: Gray Oral Reading Tests–Third Edition.* Austin: TX: Pro-Ed. Copyright © 1992 by Pro-Ed, Inc. Reprinted with permission.

Difference Score must be at least 2.5 points to reach significance ($p < .05$). Because the 5 points exceeds the 2.5-point criterion, we can say that the Rate score is significantly greater than the Accuracy score at the .05 confidence interval.

Table 3.2 *Minimum Difference Scores for GORT-3*

	Rate	Accuracy	Passage Score	Comprehension Score
Rate		2.5	—	2.7
Accuracy	2.8		—	2.8
Passage Score	—	—		2.6
Comprehension Score	2.8	3.0	2.8	

Note: Form A Difference Scores appear above the diagonal. Form B Difference Scores appear below the diagonal.

Questions:

1. Is it possible to compare a Rate Score and a Passage Score to determine if they are statistically significant? Explain.

2. What is the minimum Difference Score for the difference between Accuracy and Rate on Form A?

3. What is the minimum Difference Score for the difference between Accuracy and Rate on Form B?

4. If Jose has a Rate Score of 9 and an Accuracy Score of 11, what is his Difference Score?

5. Jose (in question 4) took Form B of the test. Is his Difference Score statistically significant?

6. Gloria took Form B of the test and obtained the following scores: Rate: 5, Accuracy: 7, Passage: 6, and Comprehension: 9. Is her Difference Score for Rate vs. Accuracy statistically significant?

7. Is Gloria's Difference Score for Rate vs. Comprehension statistically significant? (See question 6.)

8. Is Gloria's Difference Score for Passage vs. Comprehension statistically significant? (See question 6.)

9. Bob's Difference Score for Accuracy vs. Comprehension is exactly 3 on Form B. Is his Difference Score statistically significant?

10. Table 3.2 is based on significance at the "$p < .05$ level." Explain what this means.

11. In your opinion, how important is it to know whether the intra-ability Difference Scores are statistically significant? Explain.

EXERCISE 25

Use of a Bias Review Panel

Personality Assessment Inventory[1]

Guideline

The interpretation of self-report measures of personality is moderated by cultural considerations; that is, some beliefs, attitudes, and behaviors may be regarded as normative (normal or reasonable) in some cultures, while being regarded as deviant in others. Those who develop personality instruments often consider this possibility during instrument development, as indicated by the excerpt.

Background Notes

The Personality Assessment Inventory (PAI) is a self-report measure consisting of 344 items that constitute these 18 main scales: somatic complaints, anxiety, anxiety-related disorders, depression, mania, paranoia, schizophrenia, borderline features, antisocial features, alcohol problems, drug problems, aggression, suicidal ideation, stress, nonsupport, treatment rejection, dominance, and warmth.

Excerpt from the Manual

Bias Review

The history of psychometric tests has witnessed many criticisms of various instruments as unfair or unrepresentative with respect to issues of gender, culture, or other demographic features. Many of these criticisms have been justified; for example, during the 1930s a number of United States immigration quotas were based upon the results of psychometric tests that had been universally administered to different nationalities despite obvious language differences (Blanton, 1975). In the selection of final PAI items, a number of steps were taken to eliminate such bias. As a first step toward eliminating potentially problematic items, a bias review panel was assembled that represented professionals and citizens from varying backgrounds. The composition of this panel is presented in Table 7-1. These individuals were given a listing of the 1,086 preliminary PAI items and were instructed to determine whether any of these items could be perceived as offensive on the basis of gender, race, religion, or ethnic group membership. Members of the panel were asked to mark any such items and indicate the reason for their determination as a guide to revising the item. The panel identified a number of items that could be endorsed in a pathological direction because of beliefs that were normative within a particular subculture. Also, panel members identified a few items as being potentially offensive and/or confusing. All such items were deleted or revised prior to the assembly of the Alpha [final] version of the PAI.

Obviously, the utilization of a bias review panel does not guarantee that resulting items will not prove to be empirically biased. Nonetheless, it does ensure that each item has been carefully considered for bias by a group that reflects the diversity of the population likely to take this test.

Table 7-1 *Composition of the Bias Review Panel*

Black male psychologist
Black female psychologist
Black female citizen
Black male citizen
Hispanic male psychologist
Hispanic female psychologist
Hispanic female citizen
Hispanic male citizen
White male psychologist
White female psychologist
White female citizen
White male citizen
Male minister
Female minister

Questions:

1. Immigrant quotas in the 1930s were based on what?

2. Are there other groups you would like to see represented on the bias review panel?

3. What is your opinion on the use of ministers on the panel?

4. How many preliminary items did the panel review?

5. There were many more preliminary items than the final number of items selected (334). Does it surprise you that the test maker started with such a large number of preliminary items? Explain.

6. In addition to identifying items that might be offensive and/or confusing, what other types of items did they identify?

7. What did the test makers do to items that were identified by the panel?

8. The test maker notes that despite the review panel's work, the PAI still might be "empirically biased." Speculate on what "empirically biased" means.

9. In general, do you think that using a bias review panel is a good idea? Explain.

10. In addition to using a bias review panel, are there other things a test maker might do to reduce bias?

11. Based on your knowledge of tests and measurements, do you believe that bias is an important issue that should be of concern to test makers and test users? Explain.

EXERCISE 26

Pretesting Items to Reduce Bias

SRA Pictorial Reasoning Test[1]

Guideline

One approach to reducing racial/cultural bias in standardized aptitude tests is to minimize the use of language in the tests (e.g., measure the ability to reason with nonverbal materials). The rationale for this approach is that language is a major component of culture. Another approach is to try out potential test items with diverse groups and select those items that minimize differences among the groups for inclusion in the final form of the test. Both approaches are described below in the excerpt.

The excerpt also mentions part of the item analysis for the test. See the Guideline for Exercise 33 to review the purposes of item analysis. See Appendix A to review the *correlation coefficient* before attempting this exercise.

Background Notes

The SRA Pictorial Reasoning Test (PRT) contains 80 items. Each item has five pictures; four of the pictures are related in some way. Examinees are asked to identify the one picture in each item that is not related to the others. The test was designed to be a test of general ability that minimizes differences across major American cultural groups, as described in the excerpt.

The test is recommended by the publisher for predicting performance in settings that do not require previously learned reading skills.

Excerpt from the Manual

Interview Testing

Sixty items constituting the current SRA® Nonverbal Test, together with the 253 new items, were administered in an interview setting to seven American cultural subgroups of between 20 and 50 members each. The groups interviewed included Appalachians, Spanish-speaking bilinguals, rural blacks, urban blacks, urban whites, French-speaking bilingual Canadians and a control group of nonurban whites from suburbs, smaller cities and rural areas. . . . The purpose of the interview was to determine which items were ambiguous or contained unfamiliar material. During the interview, the individual was asked to respond to each item, explain his or her reasoning and comment on any picture with which he/she was unfamiliar. Pursuant to the compilation of the results of these interviews, the items were extensively edited and revised. From the possible 313 items, 270 were selected for use in the three 90-item experimental tests.

Experimental Testing

The three experimental forms were administered in an untimed format to approximately 6,000 members of the seven cultural subgroups. As a reference standard for the more difficult items, 500 college students also took the test.

A point-biserial [correlation coefficient] item analysis was performed separately for each subgroup. The final items for the test were selected to maximize two criteria simultaneously. The first was the traditional criterion of choosing those items that best discriminate between the high and low scores on the test; the second was the requirement that each item have approximately equal difficulty for every cultural subgroup. The total test thus was designed to be fair to all cultural subgroups through the selection of items that were individually, or in combination, comparable across cultures.

The experimental pool consisted of nonverbal material that was as culturally unbiased as possible. In considering mean scores of the subgroups on all 270 items, it was found that the highest-scoring group (control group of nonurban whites, 46.5) had a mean score of 31.4 percent above the lowest-scoring group (rural blacks, 35.4). After application of the criteria for item selection described above, the 80 items that now constitute the PRT had a mean for the highest group (urban whites, 53.1) that is only 8.7 percent higher than that of the lowest group (rural blacks, 48.9). These figures are based on the untimed experimental data.

Questions:

1. In addition to the seven groups mentioned in the excerpt, are there other groups you think should have been interviewed?

2. Speculate on why the nonurban whites were called the "control group."

3. What was the purpose of the interviews?

4. Do you think that the interview testing was a good idea? Explain.

5. The experimental forms were administered in an "untimed format." What do you think this means?

6. The first criterion for item selection based on the item analysis was to choose "those items that best discriminate between the high and low scores on the test." In your own words, explain what this means.

7. Is it reasonable to infer from the excerpt that all 80 items selected for the PRT were exactly equal in difficulty across all seven groups? Explain.

8. What was the lowest scoring group on both the 270 experimental items and on the 80 items selected for the PRT?

9. Does the excerpt convince you that the 80 items on the PRT are reasonably fair from a cultural point of view? Explain.

10. The data in the last paragraph are based on an untimed administration (i.e., no time limits for completing the test). In your opinion, would administration of the test with strict time limits change the fairness of the test? Explain.

11. In your opinion, should other test makers consider using the approach described in the excerpt during test construction? Explain.

12. Are there testing purposes for which reasoning tests involving language are needed in education and psychology? Explain.

EXERCISE 27

Procedures to Eliminate Bias

Stanford Achievement Test Series[1]

Guideline

Procedures for reducing or eliminating bias from tests often include making subjective judgments regarding possible bias in test items or making statistical comparisons of the performance of various groups. The excerpt shown below describes both approaches.[2] See Appendix A to review the *statistical significance* before attempting this exercise.

Background Notes

For background information on the Stanford Achievement Test Series, see Exercise 23.

Excerpt from the Manual

The issue of bias in testing began receiving proper recognition during the late 1960s and early 1970s, at which time test users and publishers became aware of the potential for bias and/or stereotyping in test materials and of the devastating effect of this phenomenon. The extent to which such bias can easily occur can hardly be overestimated. Not only is bias undesirable from a social, civil rights, and educational point of view, but it can actually result in inaccurate test scores. The issue goes far beyond such obvious things as unfair or stereotypic portrayal according to gender or race, or lack of portrayal of minority groups. Rather, some facets of bias can be so subtle as to be practically undiscernible to majority group members, whose lives have not been exposed to these facets and who therefore may not be sensitized to them. The point is that a test should not contain content that is distasteful to members of a given group or that seriously disadvantages members of any group by virtue of its greater familiarity to another group. For this reason, it is critically important that sufficient procedures be implemented during all phases of test development in order to protect against not only undesirable test content but also the presence of test items that worked differentially according to group membership.

Advisory Panel Review

The primary procedure to protect against undesirable test content involves ensuring that all test materials receive sufficient review by the proper people. An Advisory Panel of prominent minority-group educators was formed for the purpose of reviewing the Stanford 9 tryout tests for items that inadvertently reflected ethnic, gender,

---

[1]From the Technical Data Manual for the Stanford Achievement Test: Ninth Edition. Copyright © 1996 by Harcourt Brace & Company. Reprinted by permission. All rights reserved.
[2]The statistical comparisons in this excerpt are based on item difficulty. Another statistical approach to identifying bias, not shown here, is to compare the predictive validity of a test for various groups.

socioeconomic, cultural, or regional bias or stereotyping, or content that would disadvantage a group because of differences in culture or familiarity. The Panel was further asked to suggest changes or deletions based upon the presence of such items. Of the fourteen members of the Panel, four are African American, two are Hispanic, two are Asian American, two are Native American, one is Middle Eastern, one represents the Nation of Islam, one represents Home Education students, and one represents women's issues.

The fourteen members of the Advisory Panel are... [Note: The manual gives the names of the members and their institutional affiliations such as the schools or universities where they are employed.]

All Panel members were brought to a meeting at Harcourt Brace Educational Measurement to discuss and define the problem of bias. At that time, the purpose, plan, and procedures for item review were established in a workshop setting. Examples of test questions that could be considered biased or stereotyped were examined, and solutions were considered. Following this meeting, Panel members were assigned to review particular content areas and test levels based upon their stated areas of interest, their educational backgrounds, and the special needs of a particular group representation. More reviewers were assigned to the Social Science, Reading Comprehension, and Language subtests than any other subtests, due to the potential for bias that is inherent in Reading and Language passages and in Social Science items that assess history and culture. An effort was made to divide test materials equally among Panel members and to assign a particular subtest across all upper or lower levels to the same individual. The Panel members took the materials with them from the meeting in order to review them over a sufficient period of time. All materials and written comments were returned to Harcourt Brace Educational Measurement. Following this review by the Advisory Panel, items that were found to be objectionable were either eliminated from the battery or revised to eliminate the objectionable content.

Statistical Procedures

It is a fact that *individuals* differ in the knowledge and skills they bring to a testing situation. Such differences may be the result of unequal educational opportunities or any number of environmental conditions, and these differences may have an impact on achievement test results. However, an achievement test is seriously flawed to the extent that it produces differential results that reflect anything other than true differences in achievement among examinees. In particular, items that show systematic *group* differences in performance can signal the presence of bias. Tests are particularly suspect if differential results occur among cohort groups, such that membership in a group indicates that a particular examinee's scores will differ from scores of examinees in another group. Therefore, in addition to the Panel review discussed above, selected statistical procedures were used to identify items that did not fit predetermined psychometric specifications with respect to group performance.

Prior to the selection of items for the final forms of Stanford 9, all items from the tryout were analyzed according to the Mantel-Haenszel procedures, which examine differential item functioning between reference (majority) and focal (minority) groups, after matching the groups on test scores. Comparisons were made between Males and Females, Whites and African Americans, and Whites and Hispanics. An item was considered to be potentially biased if its chi-square [test of statistical significance] was greater than what would normally be expected by chance. Items showing differences greater than chance were flagged for review and possible exclusion from the final forms of the tests.

Questions:

1. According to the excerpt, are all sources of bias easy for majority group members to identify? Explain.

2. What was the "primary procedure" used to identify undesirable content in this test?

3. In your opinion, are the ethnic/racial backgrounds of the Advisory Panel members sufficiently diverse? Explain.

4. More reviewers were assigned to which three subtests? Do you agree that there is more potential for bias in these three subtests than in the subtests on mathematics and science? Explain.

5. What did the test makers do to items that were identified as objectionable by the Advisory Review Panel?

6. Here's an example of how the Mantel-Haenszel procedures work: First, match males and females to form two groups that are very similar in terms of their total Reading Comprehension scores. (Note that these two groups do *not* include all males and all females who were tested. Instead, they include only males who could be matched with females and only females who could be matched with males.) Then compare the performance of the matched groups on each individual test item. Flag all individual items that produce a statistically significant difference for possible bias.

   In your opinion, is matching an important feature of the Mantel-Haenszel procedures? Why not just compare the performance of all males with all females on the individual test items and flag those items that produce a difference? Explain.

7. Were the items that were identified by the Mantel-Haenszel procedures automatically deleted from the test? Explain.

8. Is there any other information about the steps taken to eliminate bias in the Stanford 9 that you would like to have? Explain.

9. Overall, do you think that the authors of the Stanford 9 have taken adequate steps to ensure that their test is free of bias?

Scales for Detecting Faking

Tennessee Self-Concept Scale[1]

Guideline

A potential weakness of self-report personality scales is that examinees may not respond honestly and accurately. For example, some examinees may give responses they believe are socially desirable; others may fake responses to make themselves look bad. Personality scales often include items designed to help identify such examinees. Two types are described below in the excerpt.

The excerpt refers to *T* scores. These are standardized scores that have a mean of 50 and a standard deviation of 10. Thus, a *T* score of 40 is one standard deviation below the mean, and a *T* score of 60 is one standard deviation above the mean. Since three standard deviations on each side of the mean account for almost all examinees, the effective range of *T* scores is 20 (the mean of 50 minus 3 x 10) to 80 (the mean of 50 plus 3 x 10). See Appendix A to review the *standard deviation* before attempting this exercise.

Background Notes

The Tennessee Self-Concept Scale–Second Edition (TSCS:2) is a self-report measure of self-concept. Individuals respond to self-descriptive statements using the categories "Always False," "Mostly False," "Partly False and Partly True," "Mostly True," and "Always True." It yields two overall scores: Total Self-Concept and Conflict. In addition, responses may be scored to yield sub-scores for self-concept in these areas: Physical, Moral, Personal, Family, Social, and Academic/Work.

The instrument includes four validity scales, designed to help identify examinees who are not providing accurate responses. Two of these validity scales are described in the excerpt.

Excerpt from the Manual

Inconsistent Responding

The Inconsistent Responding (INC) score indicates whether there is an unusually wide discrepancy in the individual's response to pairs of items with similar content — pairs of items such as "I am an attractive person" and "I look fine just the way I am." Such a discrepancy is often due to haphazard or careless responding. It may, on the other hand, reflect some peculiarity in the individual's life circumstances that is referred to by the content of particular item pairs. In either case, unusually high INC scores ($\geq 70\,T$) indicate that an individual's TSCS:2 profile should be interpreted with caution.

---

[1] Fitts, W. H., & Warren, W. L. *Tennessee Self-Concept Scale: Second Edition*. Material from the *Manual for the Tennessee Self-Concept Scale: Second Edition*, copyright © 1996 by Western Psychological Services. Reprinted with the permission of the publisher, Western Psychological Services, 12031 Wilshire Boulevard, Los Angeles, California 90025, USA.

Self-Criticism (SC)

The items that contribute to the Self-Criticism (SC) score are all mildly derogatory statements, such as "I get angry sometimes"—common frailties that most people would admit to when responding candidly. If the SC score is 40T or lower, the protocol may be invalid. An individual who denies most of these statements and thus obtains such a low score is being defensive and is making a deliberate effort to present a favorable picture of himself or herself. A low SC score suggests the probability that the other TSCS:2 scores are artificially elevated by this defensiveness. A low SC score does not, of course, prove faking good, because the rare angelic individual may be describing his or her typical behavior. However, the low SC score is a sign that further investigation, perhaps through interview questions or study of the client's records, should be initiated.

A score between 40T and 70T, on the other hand, generally indicates a normal, healthy openness and capacity for self-criticism. A high SC score near the upper boundary of the normal limits may reflect an actual predominance of maladaptive behaviors, such as rudeness, lying, or excessive irritability, or it may indicate the beginnings of a breakdown in typical defensive processes. Extremely high SC scores of 70T or higher signal an unusual candor or dwelling on personal faults. The client with such a high score has answered "Completely True" to all of the common frailty items that contribute to the SC score. This may indicate that the client sees little redeeming value in his or her typical behavior and has given up all attempts to regain self-esteem. The individual may be lacking in defenses and may, in fact, be pathologically undefended. The possibility of a "cry for help" or "faking bad" approach to the TSCS:2 should be considered in these cases.

Questions:

1. Suppose an examinee answered "Mostly False" to "I am an attractive person" and answered "Mostly True" to "I look fine just the way I am." Should this concern the examiner when interpreting the results? Explain.

2. What are the two possible reasons suggested in the excerpt for inconsistent responding?

3. The excerpt suggests that an examiner should be especially concerned when the T score for Inconsistent Responding is (circle one)
   A. less than 70.   B. equal to or greater than 70.

4. Is a T score of 70 a high score? Explain.

5. Consider the Self-Criticism item: "I get angry sometimes." Do you personally know anyone who could honestly answer this item with "Always False"?

6. The excerpt suggests that a T score on the SC scale needs to be how low before it triggers concern that the entire protocol (set of scores) is invalid?

7. The excerpt suggests that a T score on the SC scale needs to be how high before becoming of concern to an examiner?

8. The excerpt suggests that a very high SC score might be the result of "faking bad." Speculate on some reasons why an examinee might want to fake bad.

9. According to the excerpt, how might you further investigate a low SC score?

10. In your opinion, was the inclusion of the INC and SC scales a good idea? Explain. Do you think that one is more important than the other? Explain.

EXERCISE 29

Experiment on Faking
Survey of Interpersonal Values[1]

Guideline

One way to explore whether a self-report personality scale is subject to faking is to conduct an experiment in which examinees take the scale under different sets of instructions — such as instructions that encourage faking and instructions that do not encourage it. An experiment of this type is described below in the excerpt.

See Appendix A to review the *mean, standard deviation,* and *statistical significance* before attempting this exercise.

Background Notes

The Survey of Interpersonal Values (SIV) measures six types of values: Support (e.g., being treated with understanding), Conformity (e.g., doing what is proper), Recognition (e.g., being admired), Independence (being able to do things one's own way), Benevolence (e.g., doing things for other people), and Leadership (e.g., being in charge of other people).

Each item contains three statements; the examinee must indicate which of the three is most important to him or her and which is least important. The three statements for each item represent three of the six types of values listed in the preceding paragraph. Here's a hypothetical example to illustrate the forced-choice item format:

Indicate which of these choices is most important and which is least
important to you:
    A. doing what is proper
    B. doing things for other people
    C. being treated with understanding

Excerpt from the Manual

Sherwood Peres demonstrated that substantial distortion could be induced through the use of a strong instructional set. The SIV was administered twice to fifty-five male senior engineering students at the University of New Mexico. In the first administration, the students were asked to be completely honest and frank, as if they were in a guidance setting. In the second administration, which followed immediately, they were to assume that they were applying for a job at a prestigious neighboring electronics laboratory and were to respond as if they were really interested in the job. Significant mean differences on Support, Leadership, Conformity, and Independence were induced by the two instructional sets, presumably reflecting what these students considered to be valued characteristics of the newly employed engineer at the organization.

---

[1]Gordon, L. V. (1993). *Examiner's Manual: Survey of Interpersonal Values*–Third Edition. Copyright © 1993 by SRA/McGraw-Hill/London House. Reprinted with permission.

That the new engineering employee actually does not respond in the manner suggested by the results of the experimentally induced industrial set was demonstrated in the second phase of this study. The SIV was administered to a sample of eighty newly graduated male engineers on their first day of employment at this same electronics laboratory. Peres found the means of this employed sample to be substantially more similar to those of the seniors when responding frankly under guidance instructions, with none of the mean differences being statistically significant (Table 9). The results of this study support the position that, on the whole, individuals probably do not materially distort their responses to the SIV under normal employment conditions.

Table 9 *Comparison of Values for Engineering Students under Two Simulated Conditions and for Engineers Actually Employed*

Scale	Employment Set (ES) N = 55		Counseling Set (CS) N = 55		Employed Engineers (EE) N = 80		Mean Differences	
	Mean	S.D.	Mean	S.D.	Mean	S.D.	CS vs. ES	CS vs. EE
Support	10.3	4.8	13.2	5.3	13.1	5.3	2.9**	0.1
Conformity	20.8	5.1	13.3	5.3	11.5	5.2	−7.5**	1.8
Recognition	11.2	4.1	10.3	4.6	11.8	5.4	−0.9	−1.5
Independence	9.3	5.0	20.6	6.1	19.3	6.0	11.3**	1.3
Benevolence	15.5	5.9	13.7	6.3	14.0	6.4	−1.8	−0.3
Leadership	22.7	6.5	18.6	7.3	20.0	6.4	−4.1**	−1.4

**designates the .01 level of significance

Questions:

1. Some experts believe that the forced-choice technique described in the background notes helps reduce faking when all choices in an item are about equally desirable from a social point of view. What is your opinion of this technique? Consider the hypothetical item in the background notes while answering this question.

2. What were the engineering students asked to assume in the first administration? (Note that this is referred to as the "counseling set.")

3. What were the engineering students asked to assume in the second administration? (Note that this is referred to as the "employment set.")

4. On the average, the biggest difference between the counseling set and the employment set was obtained for which scale (i.e., value)?

5. Was the difference for question 4 statistically significant?

6. On the average, the smallest difference between the counseling set and the employment set was obtained for which scale (i.e., value)?

7. Was the difference in question 6 statistically significant?

8. Overall, were the average differences between CS and ES *or* the differences between CS and EE smaller?

9. Were any of the differences between CS and EE statistically significant?

10. Do you agree with the last sentence in the excerpt? Explain.

11. In your opinion, would it have been useful to have included a sample of engineers who were actually applying for jobs at the laboratory in addition to those who have already been hired? Explain.

12. In your opinion, would other studies in which examinees are encouraged to fake responses to other personality scales be valuable? Why? Why not?

EXERCISE 30

Social Desirability Scale

The Sixteen Personality Factor Questionnaire[1]

Guideline

When taking self-report personality scales, examinees may give socially desirable responses rather than responses that are accurate. Some personality measures have scales that help detect examinees who provide socially desirable responses.

Background Notes

The Sixteen Personality Factor Questionnaire (16PF) measures 16 primary components of personality. It also contains a social desirability scale, called the Impression Management Scale, which is described below in the excerpt.

Excerpt from the Manual

Impression Management (IM) Scale

This bipolar scale consists of 12 items. The items are scored only on the IM scale and do not contribute to any of the primary personality scales.

General Scale Meaning

IM is essentially a social-desirability scale, with high scores reflecting socially desirable responses and low scores reflecting willingness to admit undesirable attributes or behaviors. The item content reflects both socially desirable and undesirable behaviors or qualities.

Social desirability response sets include elements of self-deception as well as elements of other-deception (Conn & Rieke, 1994). Thus high scores can reflect impression management (presenting oneself to others as tending to behave in desirable ways) or they can reflect an examinee's self-image as a person who behaves in desirable ways. In both cases, the possibility exists that the socially desirable responses might be more positive than the examinee's actual behavior (i.e., a form of response distortion that may be conscious or unconscious) or that the examinee really might behave in socially desirable ways (i.e., the response choices accurately reflect the person's behavior).

Item Content/Typical Self-Report

The IM scale includes items such as "Sometimes I would like to get even rather than forgive and forget"; and "I have said things that hurt others' feelings." Answering "false" to such items contributes to a higher score on IM, indicating a socially desirable response set, whereas answering "true" indicates a willingness to admit less socially desirable behaviors. On the other hand, responding "true" to an item such as "I am always willing to help people" contributes to a higher score on IM. . . .

---

[1]Russell, M. & Karol, D. (1994). *Administrator's Manual* for the *16PF–Fifth Edition*. Copyright © 1994 by the Institute for Personality and Ability Testing, Inc. Reproduced with permission. "16PF" is a registered trademark belonging to the Institute for Personality and Ability Testing.

Use of the IM Scale

Full elaboration of the use of the IM scale is given by its authors in *The 16PF Fifth Edition Technical Manual* (see Conn & Rieke, 1994e). In brief, if an examinee's score exceeds a certain level (usually the 95th percentile for the high end of the *IM* scale and the 5th percentile for the low end), the professional should consider possible explanations for the extreme response set. For the fifth edition, raw scores of 20 or higher fall at or above the 95th percentile compared to the norm sample. . . . Depending on the reasons for testing and the criticality of accurate test data, the professional might consider retesting, especially if deliberate distortion is suspected.

Questions:

1. Briefly describe in your own words the difference between "self-deception" and "other-deception."

2. According to the excerpt, is it possible that examinees might behave in the socially desirable ways measured by the IM scale?

3. Do you know anyone who could accurately answer "false" to the statement "I have said things that hurt others" (that is, answer "false" without self-deception or other-deception)?

4. If someone answers "false" to the statement "Sometimes I would like to get even rather than forgive and forget," what effect does the answer have on the IM score?

5. If someone answers "true" to the statement "I am always willing to help people," what effect does the answer have on the IM score?

6. At the high end, what percentile rank is suggested as being of concern?

7. According to the excerpt, if an examinee scores at the 5th percentile or below, professionals should consider explanations for the extreme response set. Speculate the possible meaning(s) of such a low score.

8. Write a statement that when answered "true" by an examinee might indicate a tendency to give socially desirable responses.

9. Write a statement that when answered "false" by an examinee might indicate a tendency to give socially desirable responses.

10. On the basis of the information in the excerpt, what is your overall opinion of the IM scale? Do you think it yields valid information?

EXERCISE 31

Item Omissions and Validity

Minnesota Multiphasic Personality Inventory[1]

Guideline

When administering personality measures, we usually encourage examinees to answer all questions. To promote this behavior, the measures are generally administered without time limits so that examinees are able to consider all items at their leisure, and we often permit test administrators to give limited help (such as defining terms examinees do not understand). Despite these measures, some examinees omit some items, which complicates the interpretation of their responses.

Background Notes

"The Minnesota Multiphasic Personality Inventory-2 (MMPI-2) is a broad-band test designed to assess a number of the major patterns of personality and emotional disorders... An eighth-grade elementary-school level of reading comprehension is required..." The inventory consists of 704 true-false items.

Excerpt from the Manual

Item Omissions

Each test subject is urged to answer definitively, True or False, as many of the items in MMPI-2 as he or she possibly can. There are, of course, a number of legitimate reasons for leaving some of the items unanswered. For example, if a subject has been an orphan from an early age, he or she may not feel able to respond to items pertaining to feelings about parents. (However, many subjects will interpret such items as pertaining to foster parents or to other relatives who were like parents to them and will thus feel free to answer them. Others may take the content literally and be unable to respond.)

Some users of the MMPI have urged test subjects to guess about answers to items with which they are having difficulty. Such instructions should be avoided when administering the test although it is acceptable to request that subjects go back and reconsider items previously left unanswered. Some persons find it easier to answer the items that they left blank after they have worked their way through the whole test.

The ? (Cannot Say) score is not a scale in the usual sense; it is a simple count of the number of items that were either left unanswered or were marked both True and False by the test-taker. Since these items are not scored, they are in effect omitted from the test. As a result, the higher the Cannot Say score, the weaker any of the component scales may be to provide the desired discriminations.

---

[1]MMPI Restandardization Committee (1989). *Manual for Administration and Scoring: MMPI-2*. Minneapolis: University of Minnesota Press. Minnesota Multiphasic Personality Inventory-2. Copyright © by the Regents of the University of Minnesota 1942, 1943, 1951, 1967 (renewed 1970), 1989. Reproduced by permission of the publisher. "MMPI-2" and "Minnesota Multiphasic Personality Inventory-2" are trademarks owned by the University of Minnesota.

As indicated in Table 10, a subject may omit a large number of items for a variety of reasons. Depressed subjects may find the task of answering the items burdensome and difficult; poor readers may have difficulty comprehending some of the more complex item statements; some subjects may avoid answering items they feel are too revealing of their particular problems. All of these circumstances may lead to the omission of excessive numbers of items that cannot be scored.

Item omissions tend to lower scores in the clinical profile... If the number of items left unanswered after such urgings exceeds 30 the test record must be considered highly suspect if not completely invalid (see Table 10).

Table 10   ? (Cannot Say) Score: Implications of Score Elevations

Raw Score Level	Usefulness of Profile	Sources of Elevation	Interpretive Possibilities
High (30 & above)	Probably invalid	Severe reading problems or dyslexia Psychomotor retardation Confusion Defiance Indecision	Severe depression Obsessional state
Moderate (11–29)	Questionable validity	Mild reading problems Lack of experience Over-cautious or legalistic	Unfamiliarity with English language Paranoid mentation
Modal (2–10)	Probably valid (check content for selective omissions)	Idiosyncratic interpretation	
Low (0–1)	Valid		

Questions:

1. Describe in your own words the first legitimate reason why some subjects might omit items.

2. In your opinion, might the response format, which is True–False, lead some subjects to omit items? Explain.

3. According to the excerpt, should an examiner encourage subjects to guess in response to items?

4. In Table 10, *raw score* levels such as 11–29 are given. Explain how these raw scores are obtained.

5. Table 10 suggests that the examiner "check content for selective omissions" for a raw score level of 2–10. Speculate on what this means.

6. What raw score is associated with possible mild reading problems?

7. At what "Cannot Say" score level is the entire MMPI-2 personality profile probably invalid?

8. Severe depression is associated with what "Cannot Say" score level?

9. As you can see, omissions on a personality measure such as the MMPI-2 can be problematic. In your opinion, are omissions on an achievement test (such as a multiple-choice algebra test) equally problematic? Explain.

EXERCISE 32

Lie Scale

Minnesota Multiphasic Personality Inventory[1]

Guideline

When responding to self-report personality items, some examinees attempt to paint an untrue picture of themselves. Some personality measures have scales (sets of questions) designed to identify such examinees. The excerpt shown below describes such a scale.

Background Notes

See Exercise 31 for background information on the Minnesota Multiphasic Personality Inventory-2 (MMPI-2).

Excerpt from the Manual

Role-Playing an Idealized Personality

In completing the MMPI-2 some individuals fail to comply with the instructions to mark the items as they apply to themselves. Instead, they systematically describe someone whom they envision as having a perfect personality or an ideal adjustment. The resulting records provide poor bases for making inferences about these subjects. It is essential that some means be available to detect this approach and appraise its effects on the test patterns. Hathaway and McKinley introduced the L (Lie) scale to assess the likelihood that the test subject had approached the test with this set in mind. For this indicator, suggested by research carried out in the Harvard Character Education Inquiry by Hartshorne and May (1928) and Hartshorne, May, and Shuttleworth (1930), Hathaway and McKinley wrote items that provide the subject the opportunity to deny various minor faults and character flaws that most individuals are quite willing to acknowledge as being true of themselves. Although the L scale can reflect deceit in the test-taking situation, it cannot be viewed as a measure of any general tendency to lie, fabricate, or deceive others on the part of individuals in their day-to-day activities. Rather, it serves as one index of the likelihood that a given test protocol has been spoiled by a particular style of responding to the inventory.

As indicated in Table 11, low to average scores on the L scale indicate that the test subject was quite free of the tendency to place himself or herself in an unusually favorable light... On the other hand, very low scores on the L scale may...[reflect] a concerted effort to exaggerate emotional problems and adjustment difficulties.

---

[1]MMPI Restandardization Committee (1989). *Manual for Administration and Scoring: MMPI-2*. Minneapolis: University of Minnesota Press. Minnesota Multiphasic Personality Inventory-2. Copyright © by the Regents of the University of Minnesota 1942, 1943, 1951, 1967 (renewed 1970), 1989. Reproduced by permission of the publisher. "MMPI-2" and "Minnesota Multiphasic Personality Inventory-2" are trademarks owned by the University of Minnesota.

Moderately elevated scores on the L scale may not be indicative of a markedly defensive approach to the test but instead may reflect an individual's strongly moralistic outlook and virtuous self-constraints. In this evaluation, as in many other issues of protocol validity, it is important to have information about the test subject's prior history and background. Markedly elevated L scores very likely reflect a pervasive test-taking orientation that adversely affects the meaning of the scores on the clinical scales…

Table 11   L (Lie) Scale: Implications of Score Elevations

T Score Level	Usefulness of Profile	Sources of Elevation	Interpretive Possibilities
Very High (80 & above)	Probably invalid	Faking well-adjusted	Test resistance or naïveté
High (70–79)	Questionable validity	Random responding Denial of faults	Confusional state Repressive style Lacks insight
Moderate (60–69)	Probably valid	Defensive set	Over-conventional and conforming Moralistic Rigidly virtuous
Modal (50–59)	Valid	Typical test-taking approach	Comfortable with own self-image
Low (49 and below)	Possibly faking bad	"Plus-getting set" All True responding	Over-emphasizing pathology Self-confident and independent Cynical, sarcastic

Questions:

1. The letter "L" stands for what word?

2. Do the items in the L scale describe faults or virtues?

3. Should a high L score be taken as an indication of the examinee's tendency to lie in everyday activities?

4. Very low L scores may reflect a concerted effort to do what?

5. For L scores of 49 and below, the table suggests that examinees may be "possibly faking bad." Speculate on some reasons why examinees might "fake bad."

6. Should a score of 49 and below always be taken as an indication that an examinee is faking bad? Explain.

7. What range of L scores indicates that the profile is "probably valid"?

8. The items on the L scale describe everyday faults that most individuals are willing to acknowledge being true of themselves. An example of this type of item is "Sometimes when I am in a hurry, I accidentally drop litter and do not pick it up."[2] Answering "false" to such an item would elevate an examinees' L score. Write another item that might be used in a lie scale on a personality measure.

9. In your opinion, might it be possible for an examinee to "see through" the L scale items, mark all or almost all of them "true," yet fake his or her responses to the items that measure other traits? Explain.

10. What is your overall opinion of using scales such as the L scale to detect possible faking? If your opinion is negative, is it still better than no attempt to detect this behavior? Explain.

---

[2] This is an example of this *type* of item. It is not one of the items in the MMPI-2.

EXERCISE 33

Item Analysis: I

The Attention Deficit Disorders Evaluation Scale–Home Version[1]

Guideline

Item analysis is a statistical analysis of responses to individual items on a scale or test. Test-makers usually write many more items than they will need for the final version of their test or scale. The items are tried out with a sample of examinees, an item analysis is performed, and those items with the most satisfactory statistical properties are selected for use in the final version.

One major consideration in item analysis is the ability of each item to differentiate among examinees. It is easy to see that if all examinees get the same score on an item (such as all marking an achievement test item correctly), the item will not help identify which examinees are higher or lower than others.

Another major consideration is the correlation of individual items with the total test score. A high, positive correlation indicates that those examinees who did well on a particular item also tended to do well on the test as a whole. Clearly, it is usually desirable to select individual items for the final version of a test or scale that measure the same trait as the test as a whole. Items that do not correlate positively with total test scores may be measuring some other trait, may be ambiguous, or have other flaws.

In the excerpt, the author mentions "a strong positive skewing." This occurs when most examinees obtain relatively low scores but a scattering of them obtain high scores.

Background Notes

The Home Version of The Attention Deficit Disorders Evaluation Scale measures inattention and hyperactivity-impulsivity. Scores are obtained by having parents or guardians respond to 46 items about their child. The items describe observable behaviors, which parents rate on a scale using these choices: "Does not engage in the behavior," "One to several times per month," "One to several times per week," "One to several times per day," and "One to several times per hour." Parents are *not* asked to draw conclusions or make assumptions about their child's behavior.

Excerpt from the Manual

The item analysis of The Attention Deficit Disorders Evaluation Scale–Home Version consists of two parts:

1. An analysis of the response distribution of the items and
2. The correlation of the items within a subscale.

The first analysis indicates whether variation exists in the responses to the items. If little variation exists, the items cannot differentiate among individuals. The second part of the

---

[1]McCarney, S. *The Attention Deficit Disorders Evaluation Scale Home Version Technical Manual–Second Edition.* Copyright © 1995 by Hawthorne Educational Services, Inc., 800 Gray Oak Drive, Columbia, MO 65201; 1-800-542-1673. Reprinted with permission.

analysis indicates whether the items are measuring the same thing and whether the items discriminate between persons with high and low scores.

Analysis of Response Distributions

Inasmuch as The Attention Deficit Disorders Evaluation Scale–Home Version measures inappropriate behaviors, a strong positive skewing was expected. This does, indeed, occur; on 43 percent of the items, more than half of the subjects were assigned the lowest score (*Does Not Engage in the Behavior*); on an additional 37 percent, more subjects were assigned that answer than any other. However, there is enough of a spread among items to adequately differentiate. On all of the items, at least 19 percent of the subjects exhibited the problems at least occasionally; on 57 percent of the items, the problems were exhibited by more than half of the subjects.

Item/Total Score Correlations

The item/total score correlations for each of the two subscales of The Attention Deficit Disorders Evaluation Scale–Home Version are presented in Table 7. All of the correlations exceed .63, well above the .30 level which is considered to be acceptable.

As Lien (1976) indicated, empirical analysis should not be the sole criterion for item selection since, in some cases, the statistical selection of items can yield an assessment instrument that is unrepresentative and biased. Using Mehrens and Lehman's (1973) suggestion, the value of each item was judged as to whether it represented the characteristics to which it was assigned. If the item discriminated in a positive direction, had item to total correlation levels in a positive direction, and had acceptable content validity, the item was retained in the scale.

Table 7   *Item/Total Score Correlations*

Inattentive				Hyperactive—Impulsive			
1	.68	14	.72	22	.73	35	.76
2	.74	15	.77	23	.69	36	.76
3	.74	16	.76	24	.74	37	.78
4	.72	17	.70	25	.70	38	.80
5	.77	18	.74	26	.73	39	.77
6	.81	19	.70	27	.78	40	.76
7	.66	20	.73	28	.76	41	.66
8	.78	21	.72	29	.74	42	.67
9	.81			30	.76	43	.74
10	.73			31	.70	44	.68
11	.77			32	.80	45	.64
12	.80			33	.78	46	.63
13	.71			34	.72		

Questions:

1. On what percentage of the items did a majority of the examinees obtain the lowest score?

2. The item analysis was conducted on a broad national sample of children—not just children with attention deficit disorders. In light of this fact, would you expect a "strong positive skewing"? Explain.

3. At least 19 percent of the examinees exhibited problems at least occasionally on how many of the items?

4. The author suggests what level of item/total score correlation as being acceptable?

5. Which of the Inattentive items has the lowest correlation with total test scores?

6. Which of the Hyperactive-Impulsive item(s) has/have the highest correlation with total test scores?

7. On the basis of your answer to question 4, do all the Inattentive items have adequate item/total score correlations? Explain.

8. In addition to statistical item analysis, the author suggests that one should consider the content validity of the items. Explain in your own words what you think the author means by "content validity."

9. According to Lien, should statistical item analysis be the only criterion for selecting which items to use in the final form of a test? Why? Why not?

10. Suppose an item had a negative item/total score correlation. This would mean that people who tended to get a high score on the item tended to get a
    A. high total score.   B. low total score.

11. Explain in your own words why a test maker would be likely to discard an item with a negative item/total score correlation.

EXERCISE 34

Item Analysis: II

Comprehensive Receptive and Expressive Vocabulary Test[1]

Guideline

To review the purposes of item analysis, see the Guideline for Exercise 33. See Appendix A to review the *median* and *correlation coefficient* before attempting this exercise.

Background Notes

See Exercise 10 for information on the Comprehensive Receptive and Expressive Vocabulary Test (CREVT).

Excerpt from the Manual

Item discrimination refers to "the degree to which an item differentiates correctly among examinees in the behavior that the test is designed to measure" (Anastasi, 1988, p. 210). The point biserial correlation technique, in which each item is correlated with the total test score, was used to determine item discrimination (sometimes called discriminating power). Unfortunately, the literature gives little guidance regarding the magnitude of acceptable discriminating powers. This being the case, we applied Anastasi's (1988) suggestions regarding the interpretation of validity coefficients to the interpretation of discriminating powers. She suggests that statistically significant coefficients of .2 or .3 can be considered acceptable.

Item difficulty is the percentage of persons who pass a given item. It is used to identify items that are too easy or too difficult and to arrange items in easy-to-difficult order. Anastasi (1988) feels that an average percentage of difficulty should approximate 50% and have a fairly large dispersion. Items distributed between 15% and 85% are considered acceptable.

The item analytic procedures just described were applied to several samples of students. As a result of these analyses, good items were retained and bad items were discarded. The completed version of the Receptive Vocabulary subtest has 61 items for each form; the Expressive Vocabulary subtest has 25 items for each form.

As a final demonstration of the adequacy of the CREVT's discriminating powers and percentages of difficulty, an item analysis was undertaken using the entire normative sample as subjects. The resulting item discrimination coefficients and item difficulties are reported in Tables 7.2 and 7.3. Inspection of the summary data at the bottom of both these tables shows that the items meet Anastasi's criteria for good items.

---

[1]Wallace, G. & Hammill, D. D. (1994). *Examiner's Manual: Comprehensive Receptive and Expressive Vocabulary Test*. Austin, TX: Pro-Ed. Copyright © 1994 by Pro-Ed. Reprinted with permission.

Table 7.2 *Median Discriminating Powers for Receptive and Expressive Vocabulary (decimals omitted)*

Age Intervals	Receptive Vocabulary		Expressive Vocabulary	
	Form A	Form B	Form A	Form B
4	35	42	66	67
5	26	33	42	46
6	31	32	48	52
7	33	34	48	50
8	36	38	52	54
9	35	39	53	48
10	45	52	59	56
11	38	33	41	40
12	34	35	42	45
13	42	39	49	56
14	48	57	65	66
15	49	51	64	62
16	62	72	72	66
17	70	71	83	73
Median	37	39	52½	56
Range	26-70	32-72	41-83	40-73

Table 7.3 *Median Percentages of Difficulty for Receptive and Expressive Vocabulary (decimals omitted)*

Age Intervals	Receptive Vocabulary		Expressive Vocabulary	
	Form A	Form B	Form A	Form B
4	19	14	13	08
5	24	23	12	12
6	31	29	17	22
7	44	42	23	28
8	55	61	68	67
9	63	63	61	57
10	74	73	57	61
11	82	84	70	61
12	84	83	77	63
13	86	88	82	76
14	85	87	86	89
15	90	92	90	88
16	89	89	78	81
17	90	90	73	86
Median	78	78½	69	62
Range	19-90	14-90	12-90	08-89

Questions:

1. Table 7.2 contains median point biserial correlation coefficients *with decimals omitted*. For age 4 on Form A of the Receptive Vocabulary subtest, what is the median point biserial correlation coefficient *with the decimal*?

2. Do all of the median point biserial correlation coefficients exceed the suggested values in the first paragraph of the excerpt?

3. The median point biserial correlation coefficient for age 17 on Form B of the Expressive Vocabulary subtest is 73 (that is, .73). This indicates that those who passed individual items tended to have what type of total score? (Circle one.)

   A. A high total score.   B. A low total score.

4. On the average, what percentage of the examinees at age 4 passed the items on Form B of the Expressive Vocabulary test?

5. Overall, are the items easier at the lower age levels *or* at the higher age levels?

6. Keep in mind that the 19 in Table 7.3 for Form A of Receptive Vocabulary at age 4 is the *median* difficulty of all Form A receptive items at age 4. In light of the meaning of the term median, we know that what percentage of the items was passed by *less than* 19 percent of the age 4 examinees?

7. Is it possible to tell from Table 7.3 what percentage of examinees passed the most difficult individual item? Explain.

8. According to the excerpt, Anastasi recommends that the "average percentage of difficulty should approximate 50%." If you have a tests and measurements textbook, look up this topic and see if the authors of your book agree. Write your findings here.

9. According to the excerpt, what are the two general purposes for which item difficulty is used in test development?

EXERCISE 35

Equivalence of Editions

Self-Directed Search[1]

Guideline

Published instruments are periodically updated, which results in the publication of new editions. Whether a new edition is equivalent to the previous edition is a major concern because test users want to know whether the new edition will provide the same types of information as the edition that they have been using. Publishers usually address this issue in their test manuals.

See Appendix A to review the *mean, standard deviation, correlation coefficient*, and *percentage of variance accounted for* before attempting this exercise.

Background Notes

The Self-Directed Search (SDS) is a self-report measure designed for career counseling. It can be self-administered, self-scored, and self-interpreted. Examinees receive scores on these scales: Realistic (R), Investigative (I), Artistic (A), Social (S), Enterprising (E), or Conventional (C). The publisher provides lists of occupations that match various score profiles. For instance, the average counselor has an S,E,A profile, meaning that the Social (S) area is most important, followed by Enterprising (E), and Artistic (A). Examinees who have an S,E,A profile might consider counseling as a career option.

Excerpt from the Manual

Equivalence of Editions

The equivalence among the 1977, 1985, and 1994 editions of the SDS was estimated by comparing the means and standard deviations. . . . . In Table 28, the largest difference among editions was the mean Realistic summary score for males, which increased from 22.8 ($SD = 10.9$) in 1977 to 26.2 ($SD = 11.0$) in 1994 (a difference of 3.4). This difference and all other differences among SDS forms for each gender are always one-third of a standard deviation or less.

Two interesting observations are as follows:

1. The gender differences for the Realistic scale consistently equal one standard deviation. This difference holds despite three attempts to find R-items to which females would respond.
2. The effect of successive item revisions has been to increase R scores among both males and females, thus maintaining the gender difference. Because the sampling of subjects when developing revised editions has always been loosely structured

---

[1]Adapted and reproduced by special permission of the Publisher, Psychological Assessment Resources, Inc., Odessa, FL 33556, from the *Self-Directed Search* by John L. Holland, Ph.D. Copyright 1970, 1977, 1985, 1990, 1994 by PAR Inc. Further reproduction is prohibited without permission from PAR, Inc.

(accidental samples of high school students, college students, and adults), any interpretation of differences is hazardous.

The equivalence of the 1985 and 1994 editions was also directly assessed by administering both editions to a sample of 77 high school students (46 females and 31 males). Ideally, the two editions of the SDS should have been administered in a counterbalanced order, but this was not possible due to practical constraints. Instead, the entire sample received the 1994 edition first and the 1985 edition 11 weeks later. . . . Correlations between the summary scales of the two editions ranged from .75 to .89 [see Table 29]. These data imply that the 1985 and 1994 editions of the SDS approximate alternate forms.

Table 28 *Means and Standard Deviations for Summary Scales in the 1977, 1985, and 1994 Editions*

	Females					
	1977 (*n* = 365)		1985 (*n* = 471)		1994 (*n* = 1,600)	
Summary Scale	*M*	*SD*	*M*	*SD*	*M*	*SD*
R	12.89	7.36	14.36	7.89	14.42	8.53
I	20.51	9.59	20.47	10.12	19.05	10.27
A	20.42	10.79	23.50	10.98	22.04	10.83
S	35.41	7.44	33.56	8.78	32.37	9.76
E	26.00	10.07	26.14	10.45	24.37	10.44
C	21.28	9.56	21.27	9.69	21.94	10.75

	Males					
	1977 (*n* = 235)		1985 (*n* = 297)		1994 (*n* = 1,002)	
Summary Scale	*M*	*SD*	*M*	*SD*	*M*	*SD*
R	22.76	10.94	24.39	10.79	26.23	11.02
I	22.56	10.47	23.43	11.00	22.21	10.66
A	19.08	11.15	20.45	11.44	19.37	10.95
S	28.63	10.05	26.68	10.99	25.44	10.75
E	26.41	10.09	27.57	10.28	26.61	10.96
C	18.11	9.10	19.35	9.57	18.63	10.48

Note: Sample size varies because not all respondents completed all items.

Table 29 *Equivalence of the 1985 and 1994 Editions of SDS*

		1985		1994	
Scale	*r*	*M*	*SD*	*M*	*SD*
R	.89	18.90	12.48	17.71	12.29
I	.75	23.86	10.08	22.79	9.50
A	.83	17.37	11.18	16.71	9.11
S	.83	27.35	11.45	25.43	10.95
E	.75	23.06	11.50	22.86	10.02
C	.79	18.61	11.00	17.90	10.21

Editor's Note: Only a portion of the table is shown here.

Questions:

1. The means and standard deviations for females in 1994 in Table 28 are based on the responses of how many females?

2. In Table 28, there are more females than males for each of the three editions. Should this difference in sample size be taken into consideration when comparing the means of males and females? Explain.

3. Speculate on what the authors mean by "accidental samples." How does this affect the interpretation of Table 28?

4. On which scale in 1994 did the average female exceed the average male by the largest amount?

5. In your opinion, do the data in Table 28 suggest that the 1985 and 1994 editions are reasonably equivalent? Explain.

6. For determining the equivalence of editions, are the differences between the means in Table 28 or the differences between the means in Table 29 more relevant?

7. For which scale is the correlation between the 1985 and the 1994 editions strongest?

8. For which scale is the correlation between the 1985 and the 1994 editions weakest?

9. What percentage of the variance in the scores in the Realistic scale in the 1994 edition is accounted for by the scores on the Realistic scale in the 1985 edition?

10. Would it be reasonable to expect the correlations in Table 29 to equal 1.00? Explain.

11. Overall, what is your opinion on the equivalence of the 1985 and 1994 editions?

EXERCISE 36

Presenting Intelligence Test Items

Stanford-Binet Intelligence Scale[1]

Guideline

Examiners should carefully follow the instructions for administering tests. This is especially important when administering individually administered tests since the examiners will be interacting with the examinees and must record and determine the correctness of responses while observing and talking with examinees. As a consequence, supervised training in the administration of such tests is usually recommended. The excerpt shown below describes some issues in the administration of an IQ test.

Background Notes

The Stanford-Binet Intelligence Scale is an individually administered intelligence test. It consists of 15 tests that measure in four broad areas: Verbal Reasoning, Abstract/Visual Reasoning, Quantitative Reasoning, and Short-Term Memory. It also yields a composite IQ score that is a measure of general reasoning ability.

Excerpt from the Manual

PRESENTING ITEMS

It is crucial that you state each item exactly as indicated. In those instances where the wording of a question may be varied, the permissible alternative form is indicated. For example, the form of the questions in the Vocabulary Test may vary. Some questions, in tests such as Absurdities and Comprehension, may require follow-up probing to clarify ambiguous responses. Appropriate follow-up questions are provided in this chapter under the heading "Ambiguous Responses."

Repeating Items. If it is clear that the examinee does not understand the item or asks what is meant by it before he or she attempts a response, you may repeat the pertinent part of the item unless it is part of a memory test. This is the only procedure permissible unless an alternative form of instruction is given in the manual or item book to meet this situation. You may repeat the test question more than once if the examinee remains silent.

There are *two* other instances in which it is permissible to repeat the item or to query after an unsatisfactory response has been given: (1) if the examinee's response indicates that a part of the instruction has been misunderstood because of poor enunciation or the examinee's imperfect hearing, the entire question may be repeated. If in the Vocabulary Test, for example, an examinee defines *parrot* as an "Orange vegetable that you eat," it is likely that he or she understood you to say *carrot*; (2) if a response has been given to a word or situation that has acquired a new connotation by reason of some local or current event, query the response. However, do not give credit to a specialized response because this may change the difficulty of the item. In such a case, ask the examinee to give another meaning. For example, in the Vocabulary Test, you might say, "Yes, and can you tell me what else it means?" Only if a standard meaning of the word is given should the item be scored as passed. Under no other circumstances is it permissible to repeat the item after an unacceptable response has been given, no matter how sure you may be that the examinee is capable of answering correctly. However, except in the case of young children, repetition is not often needed and in general should be avoided.

Ambiguous Responses. A frequent source of error in testing occurs when the examiner fails to deal adequately with ambiguous responses. A response is ambiguous because the examinee has not clearly conveyed his or her meaning. Ambiguous responses cannot be scored correctly unless appropriate questioning is used to clear up the ambiguity.

Ambiguous responses are particularly likely to arise in the Vocabulary Test. A scorable response can usually be elicited by such requests as "Tell me what you mean" or "Explain what you mean." For the verbal tests, examples of ambiguous responses that should be queried appear in the expanded scoring guidelines, contained in Appendices A-E of [the test] manual, under the "Query" heading.

To be asked for further explanation of what seems obvious to the examinee sometimes elicits only a puzzled repetition of what he or she has already said. Often just a repetition of the original wording emphasizing the crucial word, "Yes, but what does *parrot* mean?" will bring results. An ambiguous response that is not further clarified by the examinee should be scored as a failure.

Follow-up Questioning. Unnecessary questioning should always be avoided. A follow-up question implies that you are in some way dissatisfied with the examinee's response. Some examinees are so sensitive to this implied lack of approval that they change their previous response. Others may be discouraged from making further efforts to clarify their responses. Acceptance of the first response while asking for further clarification tends to dispel this implication of disapproval. For example, if an examinee defines *envelope* as "like a letter," say "Yes, but what else does *envelope* mean?" Thorough familiarity with the scoring standards will be of great advantage in making the necessary on-the-spot evaluation of ambiguous responses. Just which follow-up question to use depends on the context and what kind of clarification is needed. How many follow-up questions to use has to be more or less a matter of judgment. If one follow-up question does not suffice, continue your efforts to determine to your satisfaction whether the examinee knows the correct response.

Questions:

1. An examiner should *not* repeat the item (or pertinent part of the item) even if the examinee does not understand it on what type of test?

2. If an examinee remains silent after a question is asked, the examiner may do what?

3. If the examiner poorly pronounces a word, what may the examiner do?

4. What should an examiner do if an examinee defines *book* as "to see," which may mean that he or she thought the examiner said *look*?

5. What are the suggested words an examiner might use to request the clarification of an ambiguous response?

6. How should an examiner score an item that elicits an ambiguous response that is not clarified by the examinee?

7. What does follow-up questioning imply?

8. Does the excerpt indicate how many follow-up questions may be asked about an item?

9. Overall, do you think that the presentation of items on the Stanford-Binet is subjective? (Circle one and justify your answer.)

   A. Yes. It is very subjective.
   B. It is somewhat subjective/somewhat objective.
   C. No. It is very objective.

10. In light of the excerpt, do you think that people who wish to administer the Stanford-Binet should have specialized training with practice sessions on administering it? Explain.

EXERCISE 37

Testing Conditions

Minnesota Multiphasic Personality Inventory[1]

Guideline

Most standardized measures come with instructions on how to establish proper testing conditions for administering a particular test. The excerpt shown below is an example.

Background Notes

See Exercise 31 for background information on the Minnesota Multiphasic Personality Inventory-2 (MMPI-2).

Excerpt from the Manual

Testing Conditions

The typical testing situation for administering the MMPI-2 requires adequate space at a table to lay out the test booklet and answer sheet, good lighting, a comfortable chair, and quiet surroundings free of intrusions and distractions. However, it is often not possible to provide an ideal testing environment. For example, the hardcover version permits the test subject to take the test in a waiting room or while sitting up in bed in a hospital ward. In such settings precautions must be taken to ensure that the person taking the test is not bothered by others in the room or offered gratuitous advice by fellow patients. It is generally permissible to let the subject take the test during limited time intervals, say, before and after an interruption for routine procedures.

Administration to large groups requires special measures to ensure maximal cooperation and care in completing the test. In a small group, the person administering the test may function as proctor. However, most examiners prefer to have at least one other person helping. Generally one additional proctor may be needed for each 20 to 25 subjects. Special conditions in the testing room, such as testing younger subjects in a crowded room, may make additional help necessary. It is also usually necessary under such circumstances to have one or more individuals in attendance who are acquainted with the young men and women by name and who can exercise effective control over them to ensure cooperation and proper attention to the test.

Those who assist in the testing session must conduct themselves in the same serious and professionally mature manner recommended for the examiner. Proctors accustomed to the close supervision required in timed ability testing should be explicitly instructed to be more circumspect. During the administration of a personality inventory like the

---

[1]MMPI Restandardization Committee (1989). *Manual for Administration and Scoring: MMPI-2.* Minneapolis: University of Minnesota Press. Minnesota Multiphasic Personality Inventory-2. Copyright © by the Regents of the University of Minnesota 1942, 1943, 1951, 1967 (renewed 1970), 1989. Reproduced by permission of the publisher. "MMPI-2" and "Minnesota Multiphasic Personality Inventory-2" are trademarks owned by the University of Minnesota.

MMPI-2, sensitive subjects may interpret even quite casual conversations between proctors as a discussion of their replies to the test items. Similarly, lingering too long in one place in the room may be interpreted as undue curiosity about what the subjects in that area are endorsing. Only enough attention to detect marking errors, lack of persistence, or actual copying of answers should be given.

Some test subjects may react aloud to the content of some of the items and provoke a series of comments from others which can be disruptive if not headed off early. Proctors may often be asked to clarify the content or referents of particular items; they should be instructed to give simple definitions of words and to rephrase colloquialisms or idioms; extended discussion should be avoided. Usually it is sufficient to say, "Just indicate the way that you see it."

Questions:

1. Is it necessary for the examiner to always provide a table and chair for the subjects who are taking the inventory? Explain.

2. Should the inventory always be taken during a single time period or may it be administered across several time periods? Explain.

3. What do the authors mean by "gratuitous advice"?

4. It is necessary to have someone present who knows the subjects by name under what circumstances?

5. How might sensitive subjects interpret even casual conversations among the proctors?

6. What is the problem with having proctors linger near an examinee while he or she is taking the inventory?

7. Should a proctor expect to be asked to clarify the meaning of items? Are the proctors permitted to do so? Explain.

8. In the last paragraph of the excerpt, the authors suggest "heading off" comments that subjects make aloud. How would you do this if you were a proctor?

9. The excerpt contains the complete passage on testing conditions included in the manual for the MMPI-2. Is this topic covered in full and to your satisfaction? Explain.

EXERCISE 38

Establishing Rapport During Test Administration

Woodcock-Johnson Revised Tests of Cognitive Ability[1]

Guideline

Establishing rapport between an examinee and the test administrator, who is often a stranger to the examinee, is especially important when using individually administered tests. When taking such tests, examinees may view any comments or nonverbal gestures made by the test administrator as a reflection on them and their performance. Unless the test administrator acts appropriately, the examinee may feel uncomfortable and not perform at his or her optimum level. Many test manuals provide guidance on this issue. The excerpt shown below is an example.

Background Notes

The standard version of the Woodcock-Johnson Revised Tests of Cognitive Ability consists of seven tests of children's intellectual ability: Memory for Names, Memory for Sentences, Visual Matching, Incomplete Words, Visual Closure, Picture Vocabulary, and Analysis-Synthesis. It is individually administered.

Excerpt from the Manual

You will have little difficulty establishing a good testing relationship with most subjects. Do not begin testing unless the subject seems relatively at ease. If a subject does not feel well, do not attempt testing. During the test, give the impression that administering the test to the subject is an enjoyable experience. Smiling frequently and calling the subject by name help to maintain a pleasant testing environment. You may wish to begin the testing session with a short period of conversation, perhaps while completing the subject information portion of the Test Record [where the administrator records information such as the examinee's date of birth and grade level]. Do not give a lengthy explanation of the test or apologize for giving the test. A suggested statement to introduce the test is provided in the introductory section of each Test Book labeled "Introducing the Test."

Enhance rapport throughout the testing session by frequently letting the subject know that he or she is doing a good job, using such comments as "fine" and "good." Encourage the subject to respond even when items are difficult. Be careful that your pattern of comments does not indicate whether answers are correct or incorrect. Habits to avoid include saying "good" only after correct responses, or pausing longer after incorrect responses as if expecting the subject to change the first response.

Questions:

1. According to the excerpt, should you provide a lengthy discussion of the test and its purposes in order to make the examinee comfortable before beginning the test?

2. The excerpt suggests beginning the testing session with a short period of conversation. Suppose you were testing a third grader. How would you initiate such a conversation? (Be specific.) If you would ask the child some questions about himself or herself, what questions would you ask?

3. In your opinion, is it a good idea to hold the conversation mentioned in question 2 while you are filling out the Test Record as suggested in the excerpt? Would it be better to give the child your undivided attention while holding the conversation?

4. According to the excerpt, is it acceptable to let the subject know that he or she is doing a good job on the test?

5. The excerpt *implies* that the administrator should occasionally say "good" after both correct *and* incorrect responses by an examinee. What is your opinion on saying "good" after an incorrect response? Does it pose an ethical problem for you? Are any ethical considerations outweighed by the possible benefit of doing this?

6. The excerpt indicates that a test administrator should encourage an examinee to respond to difficult test items. Suppose you were administering the test to a fourth grader for whom many of the items were difficult. What would you do or what would you say to encourage responses?

7. What warning is given about pausing after an examinee gives responses?

8. Speculate on why the test administrator should avoid giving hints as to whether a response is correct or incorrect.

9. Do you think that the excerpt gives you sufficient information on how to establish rapport? Do you have any unanswered questions about how to do this? Explain.

EXERCISE 39

Responsibility for Test Security

Woodcock Language Proficiency Battery[1]

Guideline

If examinees have prior knowledge of the specific items on a test or the correct answers, their scores will be invalid. The excerpt shown below illustrates how one test maker describes the test users' responsibilities for keeping test materials secure.

Background Notes

The Woodcock Language Proficiency Battery-Revised (WLPB-R) contains tests in Oral Language (such as Memory for Sentences and Picture Vocabulary), Reading (such as Letter-Word Identification and Passage Comprehension), and Written Language (such as Dictation and Proofing).

Excerpt from the Manual

Test security is the responsibility of test users (including examiners, program administrators, and others). Prior knowledge of test content may invalidate the scores of potential subjects. Test security has two aspects: The first regards storing test materials; the second relates to providing information about the content of specific test items. Tests such as the WLPB-R should be kept in locked cabinets if stored in an area accessible to people with a nonprofessional interest in the tests. For example, the test should not be left unattended in a school building where students might see the materials and look at the test items.

During the discussion of test results with a subject or with a subject's parents, you may describe the nature of the items included in a test, but avoid actual review of specific test content. In most cases, it is easy to think of similar examples of test items without revealing specific items.

The issue of test confidentiality is an important one to bear in mind. Do not share test content with curious nonprofessionals who may not appreciate the importance of test confidentiality. Some have argued that test materials should be made available for public inspection. Others argue that a subject should be shown the test questions, his or her answers, and the correct answers following any testing. These practices may be acceptable with certain kinds of tests in special situations. They are, however, completely unacceptable practices in the case of irreplaceable tests such as those of the WLPB-R battery, which can have their validity quickly destroyed by disclosure. As noted on the copyright page of this manual, the WLPB-R is not to be used in any program that follows such practices. *Standards for Educational and Psychological Testing* [APA (American Psychological Association), 1985] states:

Standard 15. 7

Test users should protect the security of test materials.

Those who have test materials under their control should take all steps necessary to ensure that only individuals with a legitimate need for access to test materials are able to obtain such access.

Questions:

1. What are the two major aspects of test security?

2. Suppose the tests were to be stored in the school counselor's office? Would you recommend that they be stored in a *locked* cabinet? Explain.

3. Suppose a parent is inquiring about his or her child's low score on Passage Comprehension. According to the excerpt, would it be acceptable to show the parent a couple of sample items from the test? Explain.

4. After testing, is it acceptable to show an examinee the test questions on this test, his or her answers, and the correct answers (according to the excerpt)?

5. The test makers note that some have argued that test materials should be made available for public inspection. Clearly, the test makers disagree—at least with respect to the WLPB-R. What is your position on this issue? Explain.

6. Suppose a test user thinks that the contents of this test should be made public. Are there any legal reasons why such a person should not make it public?

7. Suppose a test user thinks that the contents of this test should be made public. Would it be unethical for such a person to make them public? Explain.

Appendix A[1]

Review of Basic Statistics

This appendix provides a brief review of statistics that are widely reported in test manuals. It is designed only to remind you of the highlights that you will need while answering the questions in this book. You should refer to a more comprehensive treatment in your tests and measurements book or a statistics book if you have not previously studied statistics.

Mean: The most popular average. (Test makers usually use the symbol M for the mean in test manuals.) It is obtained by summing a set of scores and dividing by the number of scores. Here's an example:

- Scores: 3, 4, 5, 6, 7, 9, 10
- Sum of the scores: 44
- Sum of the scores (44) divided by the number of scores (7) = 6.3, which is the mean.

The mean is sensitive to extreme scores: A relatively small number of very high scores can pull it up, or a relatively small number of very low scores can pull it down. Here's an example using the same scores as in the first example but adding one examinee who has a very high score of 95:

- Scores: 3, 4, 5, 6, 7, 9, 10, 95
- Sum of the scores: 139
- Sum of the scores (139) divided by the number of scores (8) = 17.4.

Notice that the addition of just one examinee with a very high score has almost tripled the value of the mean. Since none of the examinees scored close to 17.4, the mean in this example is not a good representation of the average. When there are small numbers of extremely high or low scores, test makers tend to use a different average—the *median*.

Median: An average; compare with the *mean* above. (Test makers usually spell out its name rather than using a symbol for it in test manuals.) It is the "middle score"; that is, it is the score that half the examinees are higher than and half the examinees are lower than. Here's an example we considered while discussing the *mean*. In this example, the median is 6 because half the examinees scored higher than 6 and half scored lower than 6:

Scores: 3, 4, 5, 6, 7, 9, 10
↑

Unlike the *mean*, the median is insensitive to extreme scores, which makes it a good alternative to the mean when there are such scores in a distribution. Below is another example we considered while discussing the *mean*. In this example, there is one

---

[1]Mildred L. Patten and Zealure C. Holcomb assisted in the preparation of this appendix.

examinee with a very high score of 95. However, this examinee with an extreme score has little effect on the value of the median, which is 6.5 (half way between the middle scores of 6 and 7).

Scores: 3, 4, 5, 6, 7, 9, 10, 95
↑

Thus, test makers tend to use the median as the average when there are small numbers of extremely high or low scores.

Standard Deviation: A measure of variability. (Test makers usually use the symbol S or SD to stand for the standard deviation in test manuals.) It indicates the extent to which examinees differ from the mean of their group. For example, consider these scores:

15, 15, 15, 15, 15, 15, 15

Their mean is 15.00. Since all examinees are exactly at the mean, their standard deviation is 0.00.

Standard deviations are greater than zero when examinees differ from the mean, as illustrated by the next two examples. In both cases, the mean is 15 but the scores with the larger standard deviation have greater differences between the scores and the mean.

14, 14, 14, 15, 16, 16, 16
The standard deviation equals 0.93

0, 5, 10, 15, 20, 25, 30
The standard deviation equals 10.00. You should be able to see that there is greater variation (i.e., larger differences) in this set of scores than in the previous two sets of scores. The larger variation is reflected in the larger standard deviation.

It is beyond the scope of this brief appendix to illustrate the computation of the standard deviation. The relationship between the standard deviation and the normal curve (symmetrical, bell-shaped curve) is illustrated in some of the exercises in this book.

Correlation Coefficient: A measure of relationship. (Test makers usually use the symbol r to stand for the correlation coefficient in test manuals.) It measures the extent to which two measures put examinees in the same order. Consider Table 1, where the examinees are *roughly* in the same order. That is, people like Joe and Jane who have high employment test scores have high ratings by their supervisor on the job; people like Jake and John, who have low employment test scores have low supervisor's ratings. The value of r for these data is .89.

Table 1 *Scores with a Strong Relationship (r = .89)*

Employee	Employment Test Scores	Supervisor's Ratings
Joe	35	9
Jane	32	10
Bob	29	8
June	27	8
Leslie	25	7
Homer	22	8
Milly	21	6
Jake	18	4
John	15	5

Correlation coefficients *found in test manuals* usually range between 0.00 (no relationship) and 1.00 (a perfect relationship). Although there are no universal rules for interpreting correlation coefficients, it would be fair to say that those below .30 would tend to be called "weak" or "very weak," those between .31 and .59 would tend to be called "moderate," and those that are .61 or higher would tend to be called "strong" or "very strong."

It is also possible for a correlation coefficient to be negative, indicating an inverse relationship (that is, those who are high on one measure are low on the other). If a relationship is perfectly inverse, the value of *r* is –1.00. Negative correlations are rare in test manuals. When they are found, they are usually in relation to personality variables. For example, we would get a negative correlation if those who score high on a depression scale score low on a cheerfulness scale and vice versa.

When correlation coefficients are used to describe the validity of a test, they are often called *validity coefficients*. When they are used to describe reliability, they are often called *reliability coefficients*.

Note that there are special forms of correlation sometimes mentioned in test manuals (such as the *biserial correlation coefficient*). For the typical consumer of tests, it is sufficient to interpret these in the same way the basic correlation coefficient is interpreted.

Percentage of Variance Accounted For: A statistic used to interpret correlation coefficients. Consider the employment scores in Table 1 above. There you see variance in the scores (that is, differences among the scores). A test maker would be concerned with the extent to which the variance on the employment test scores *accounts for* or predicts the variance in the supervisor's ratings.

To get the *percentage of variance accounted for*, simply square the correlation coefficient (in this case, .89), multiply by 100, and add a percentage sign. Thus:

$$.89 \times .89 = .79 \times 100 = 79\%$$

Thus, we can say that 79% of the variance in supervisor's ratings is accounted for by the variance in employment test scores. For perfect prediction, the percentage of variance accounted for would have to equal 100%.

Statistical Significance: When we declare a difference to be statistically significant, we are saying that it is unlikely that the difference was created by random (chance) errors. For example, we might test a random sample of boys and a random sample of the girls in a school district and compute the mean for each group. The difference between the means that we observe in the samples may be due to the errors created by random sampling. That is, random sampling may have given us unrepresentative samples of boys and girls, and this lack of representativeness may have caused an apparent (incorrect) difference. In addition to sampling, random measurement errors can be created by testing, such as careless marking, guessing by examinees, and by a test maker's selecting just a small sample of all the possible content to include in a test.

By performing what are known as significance tests (using mathematical procedures that are beyond the scope of this book), test makers can determine the probability that random errors created a particular difference. Usually, test makers declare statistical significance when the probability (*p*) that random errors created the difference is equal to or less than 5 in 100; this is expressed as $p < .05$.

When a test maker declares a correlation coefficient to be statistically significant, he or she is saying that the value obtained is significantly greater than 0.00. In other words, if you read that a correlation coefficient of .49 is statistically significant at the .05 level, you would know that there are 5 or fewer chances in 100 that random errors would create a correlation of .49 if *in truth* (without random errors) the real correlation is 0.00.

To put it simply, when you read in this book that a difference is statistically significant, you will know that a significance test led a test maker to believe that it was not created by random errors.

Notes:

Notes:

Notes:

Notes: